ANIMALS DOING VERY HUMAN THINGS

&

REPTILES!

COLORING BOOK

2 BOOK BUNDLE

ANIMALS
Doing Very Human Things
Coloring Book

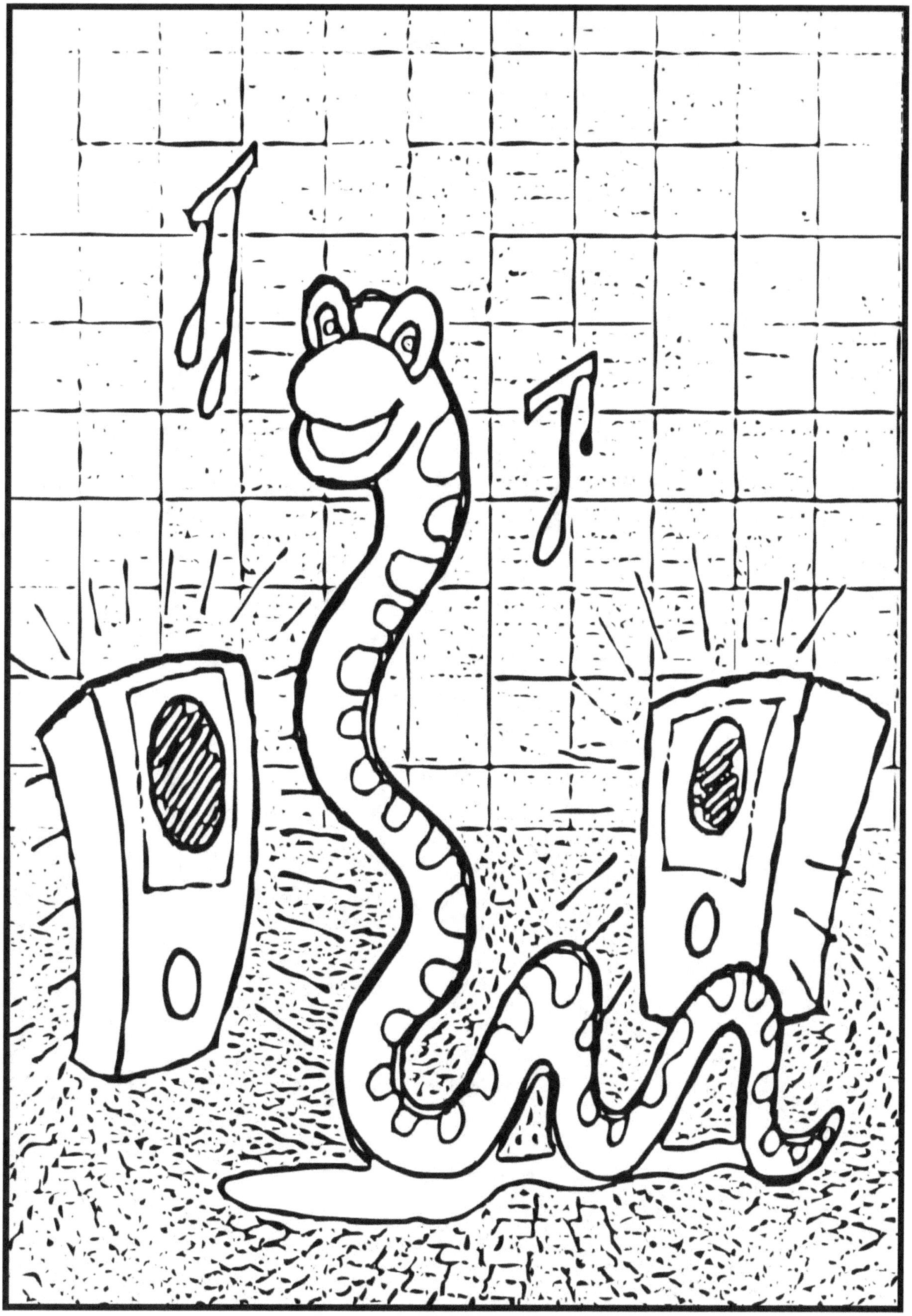

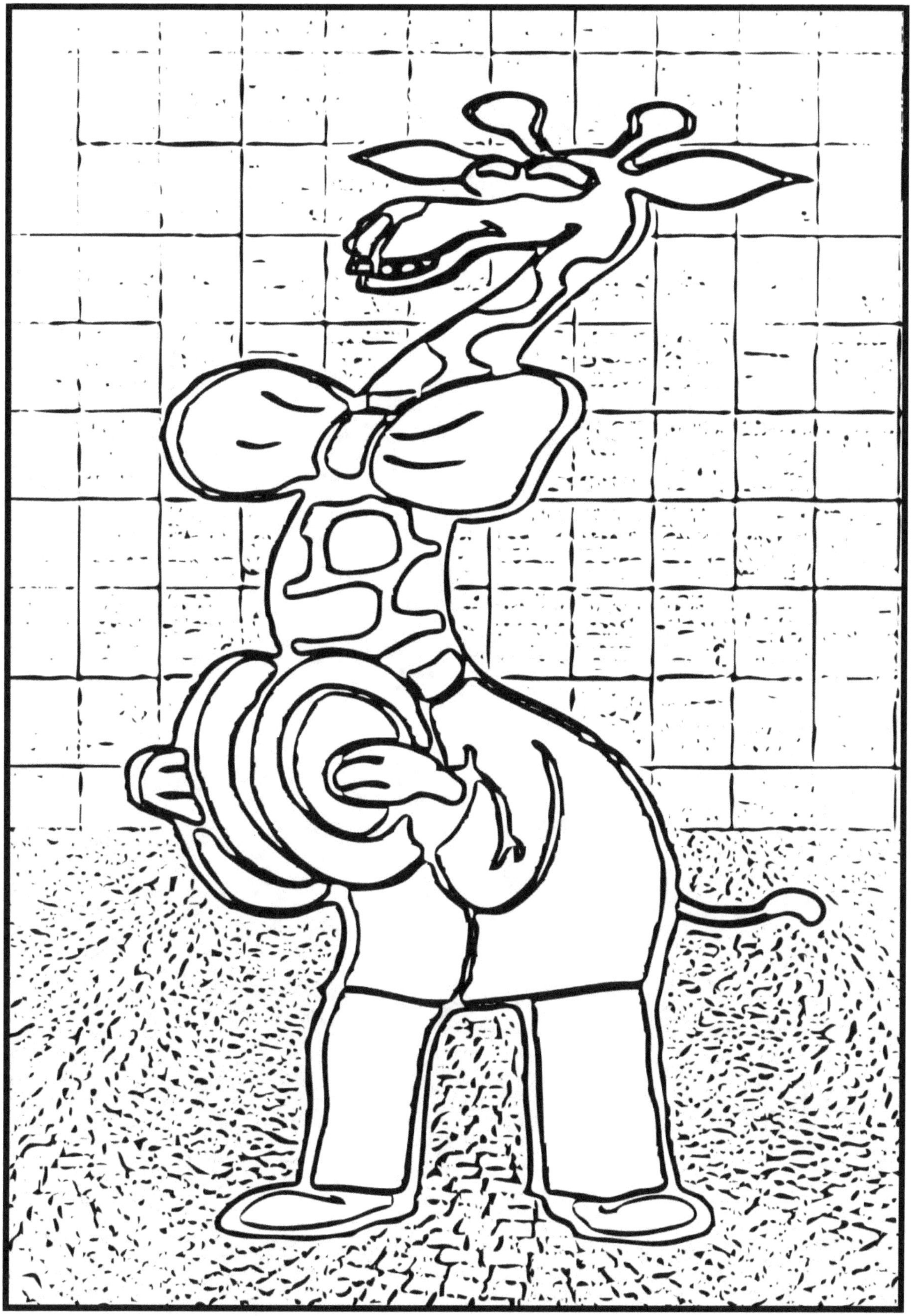

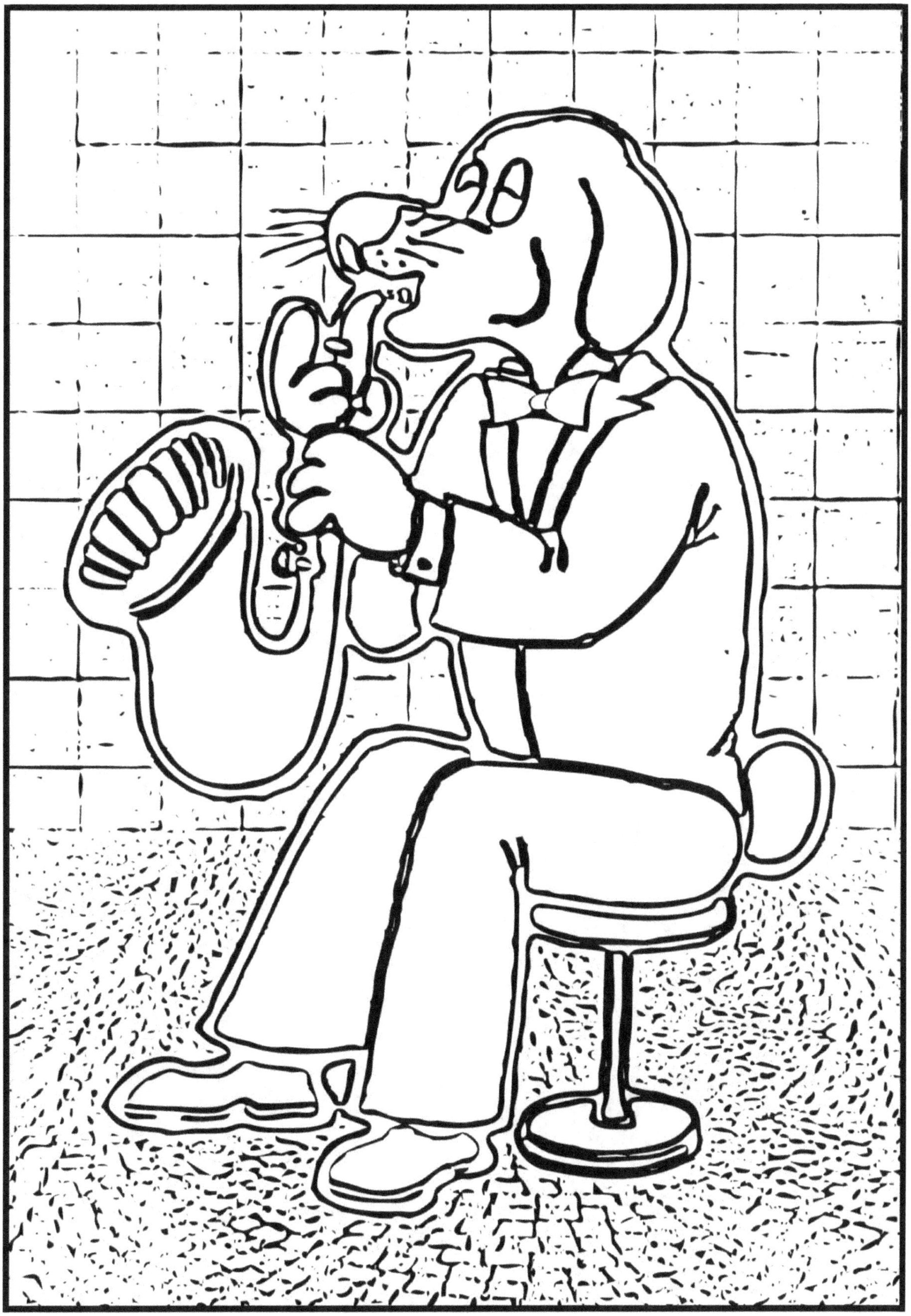

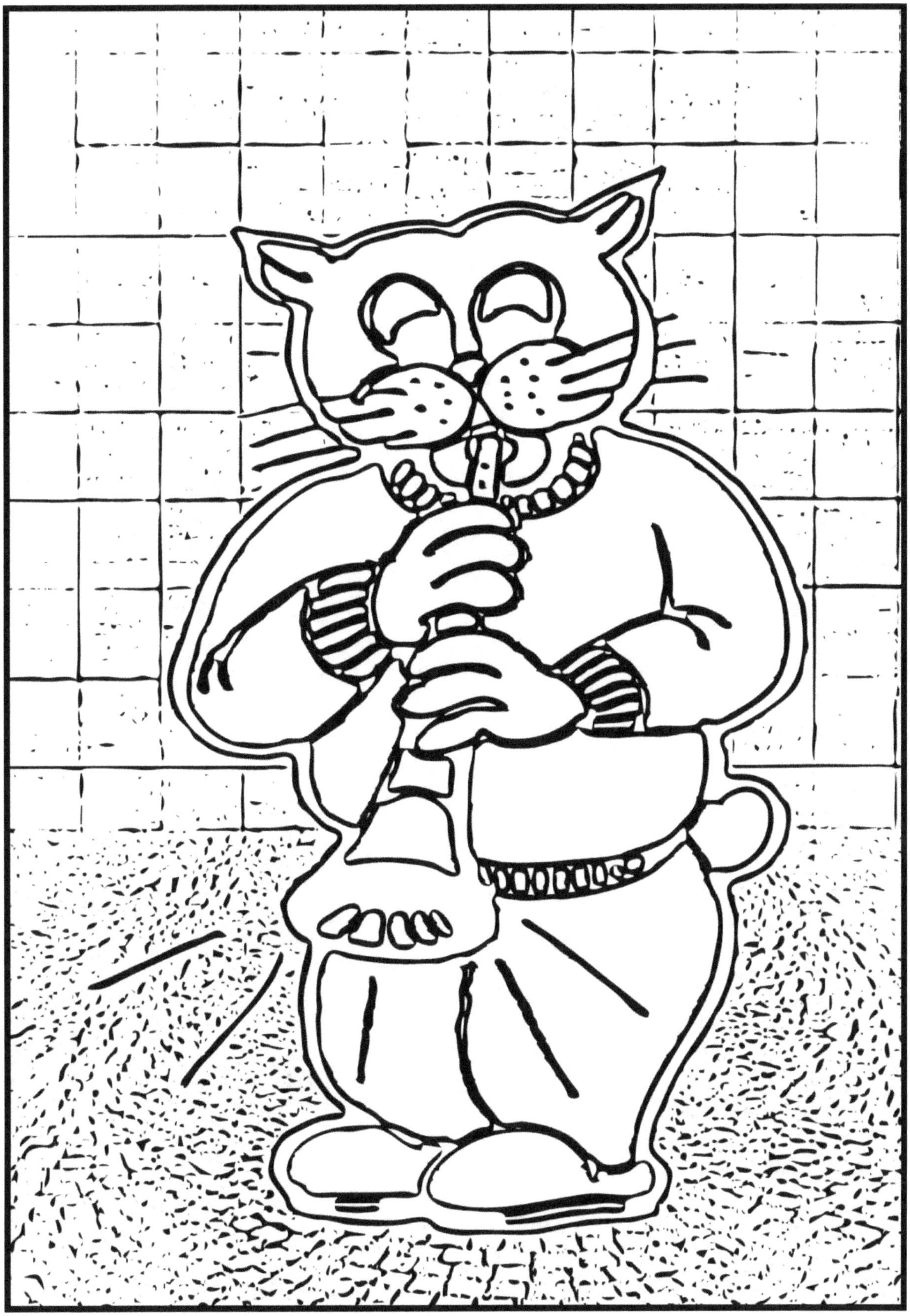

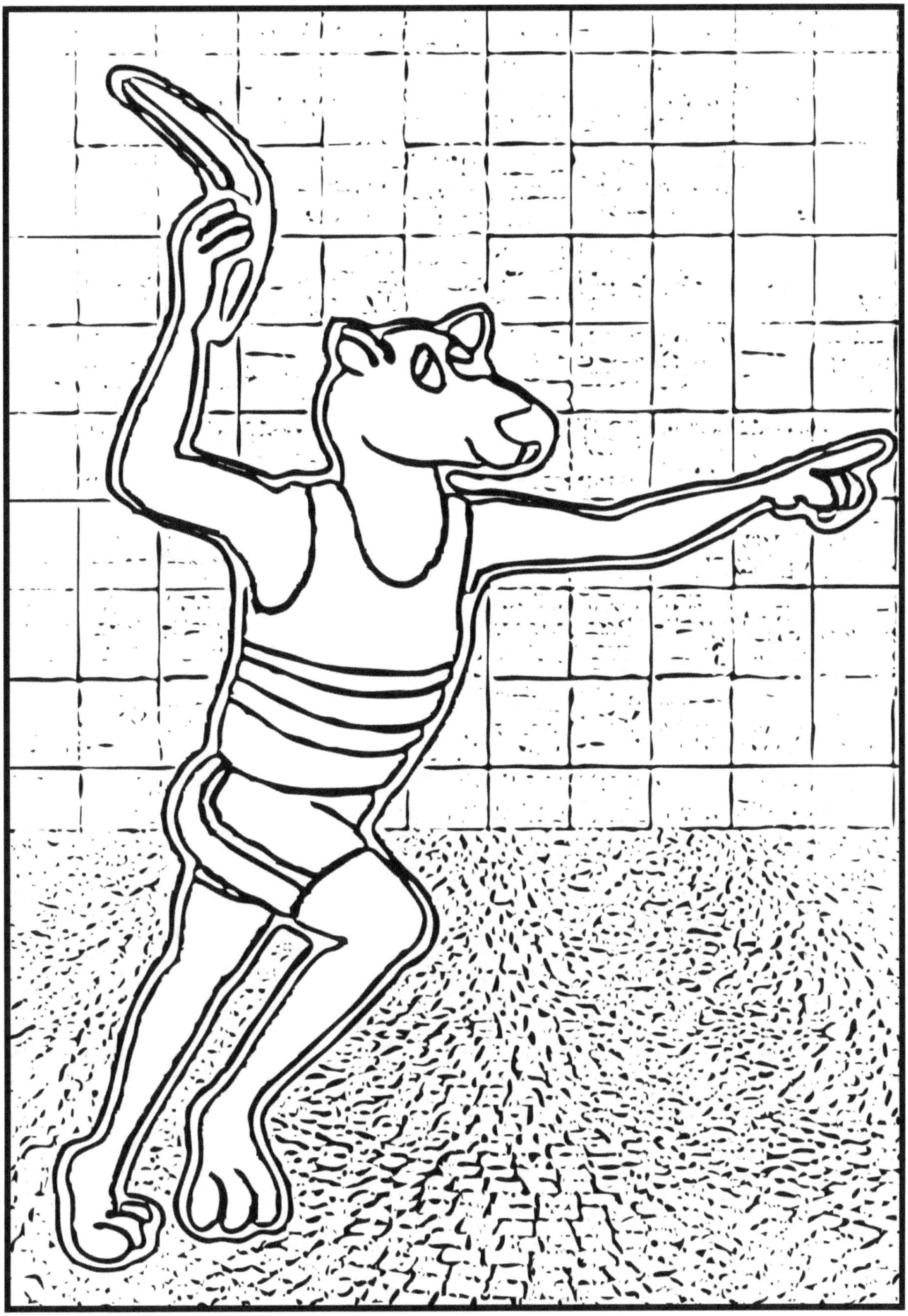

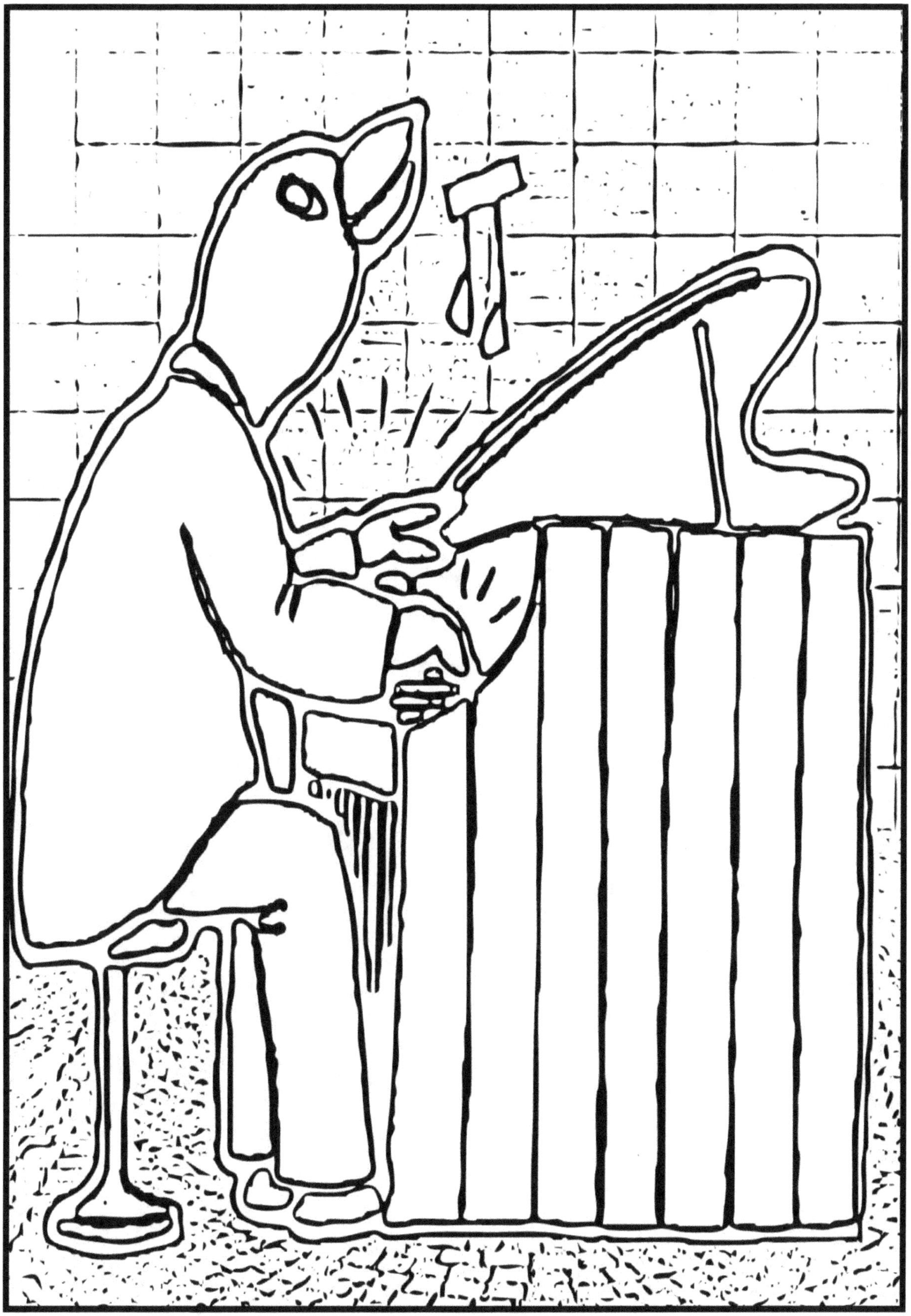

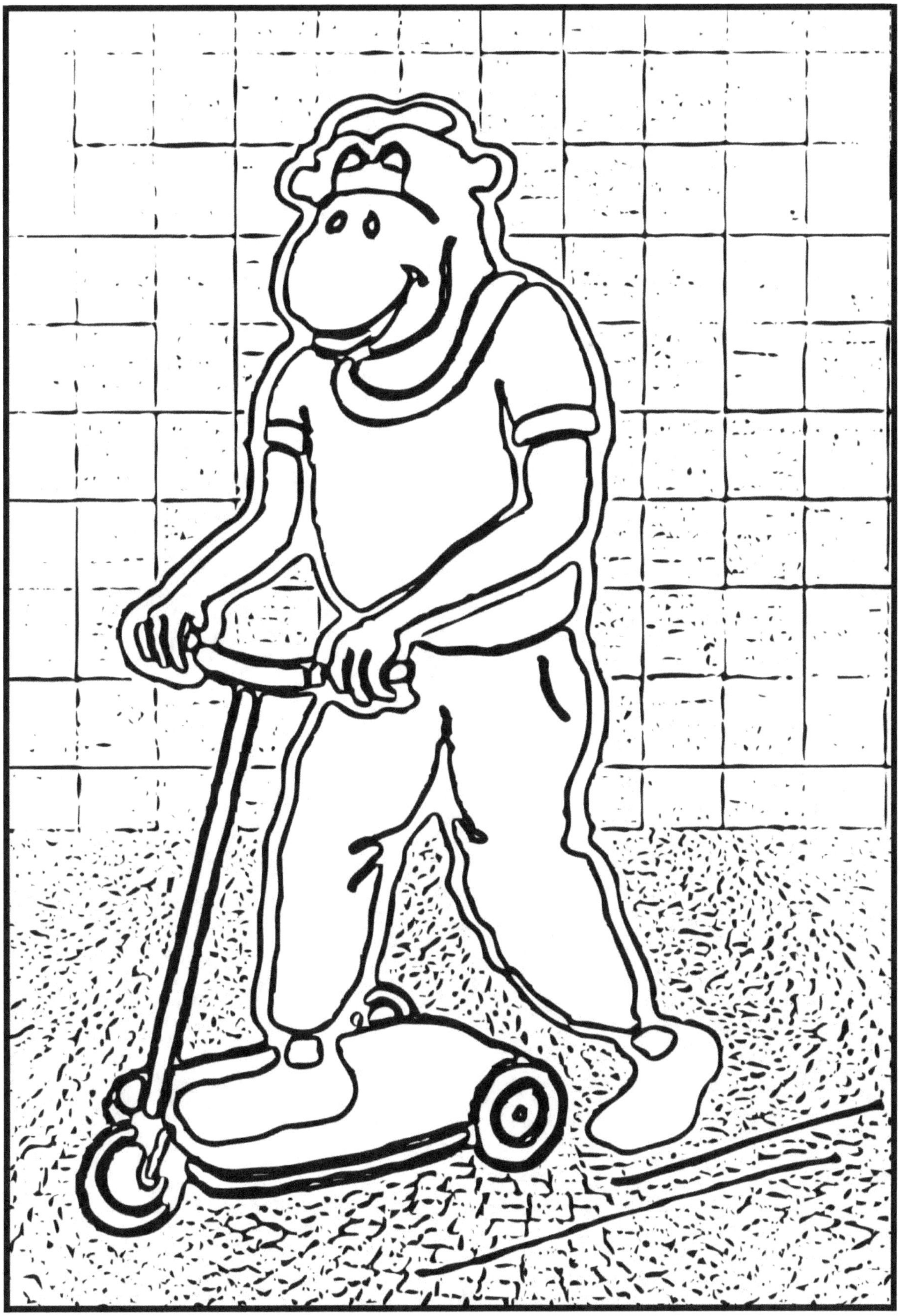

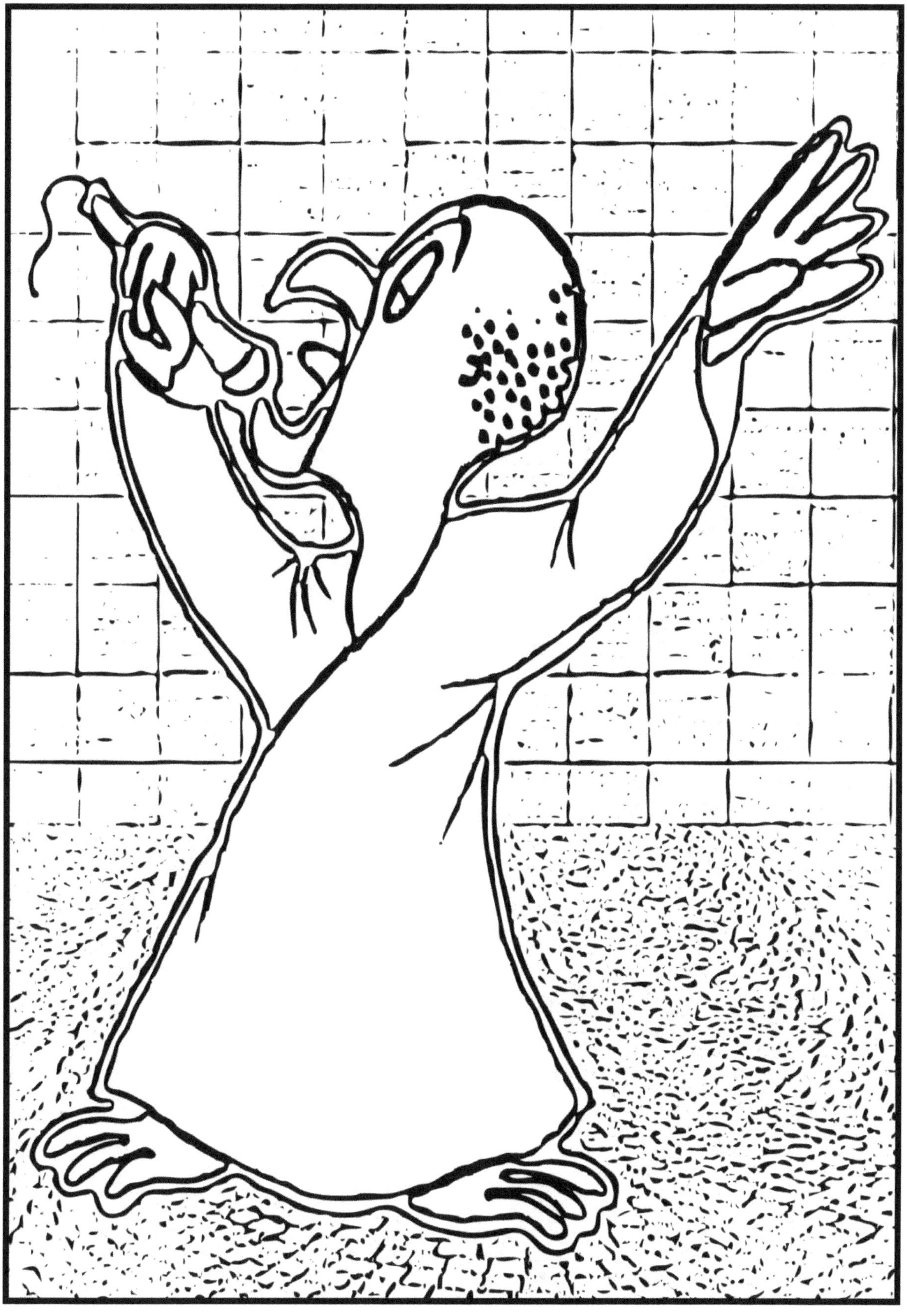

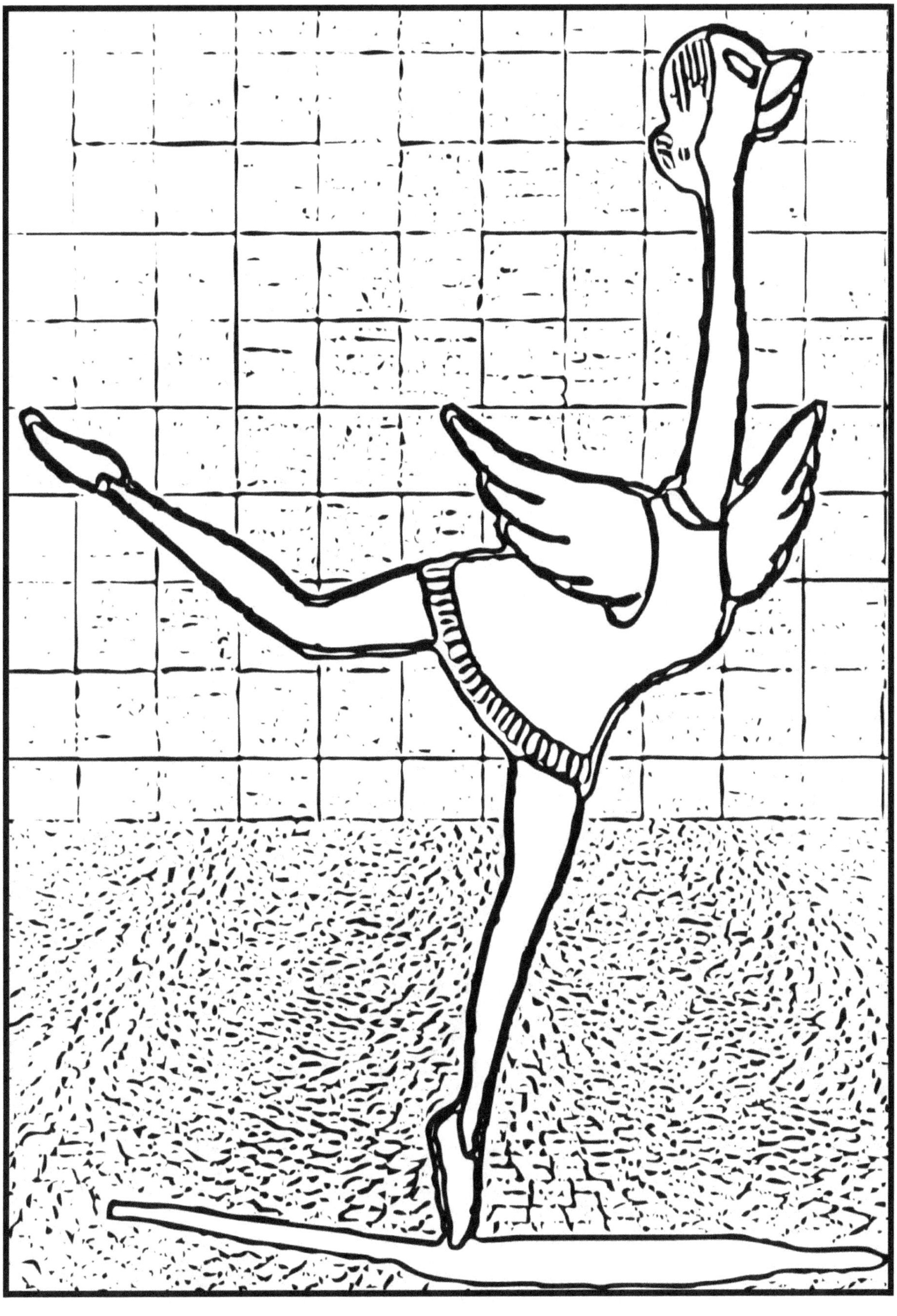

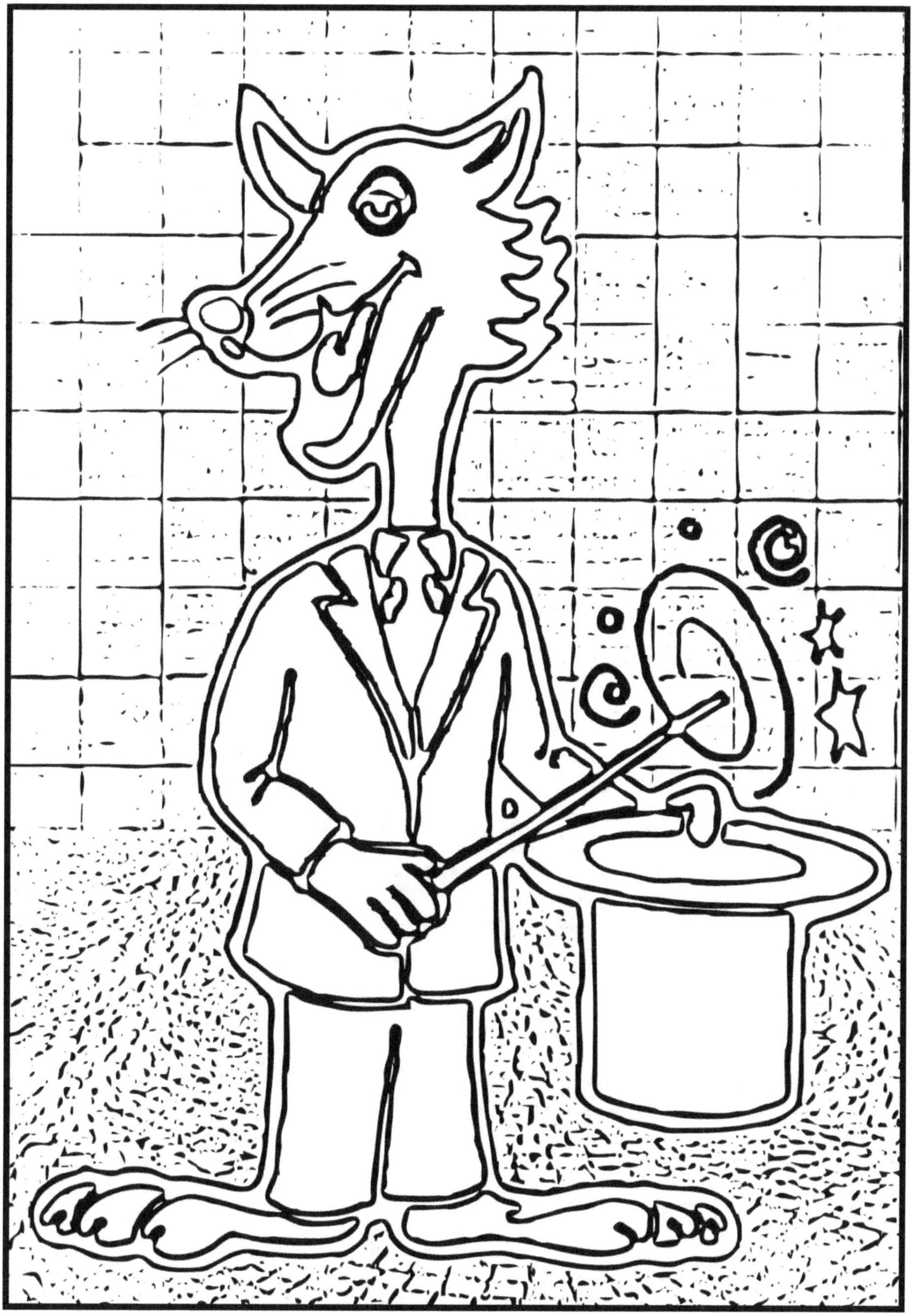

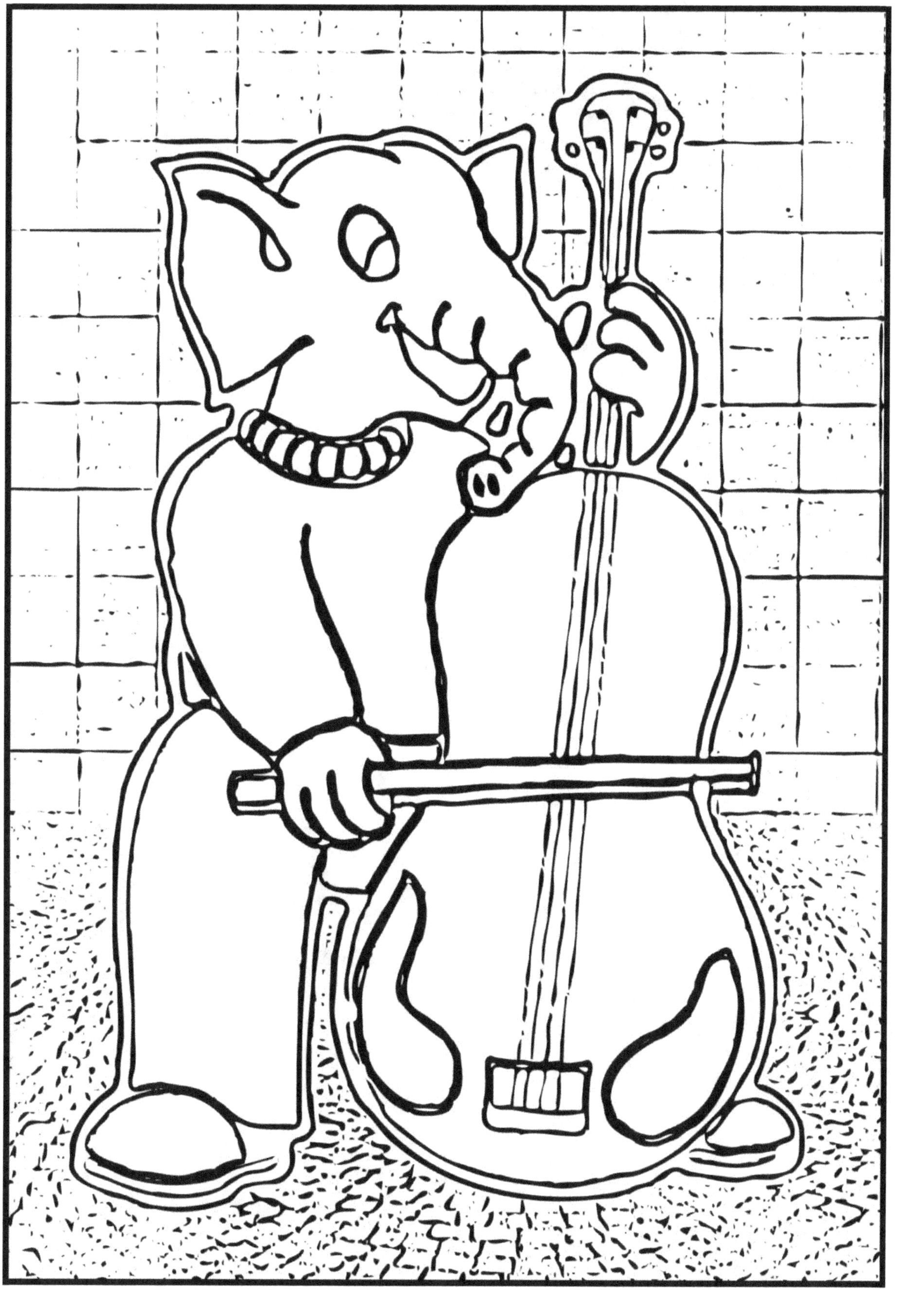

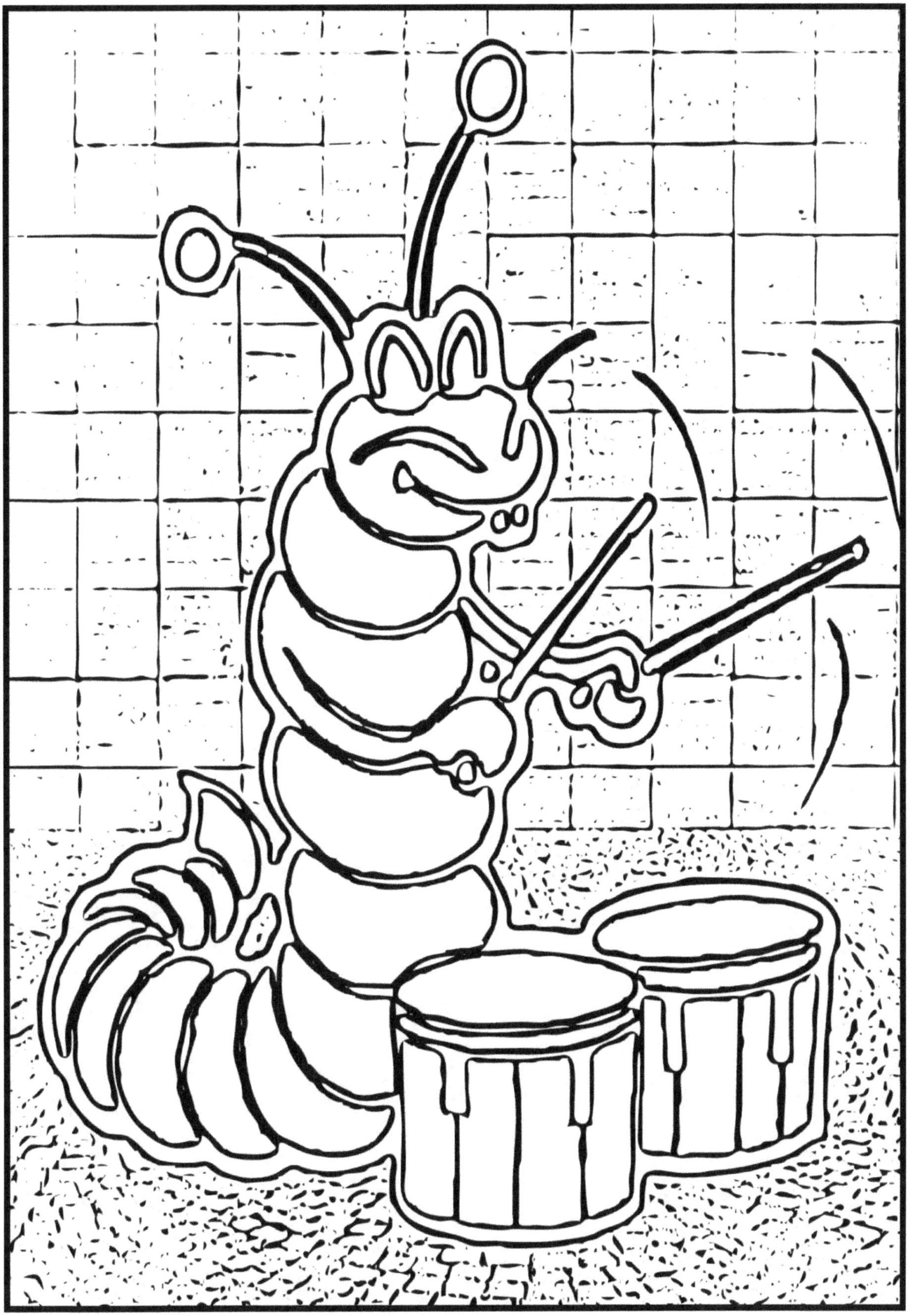

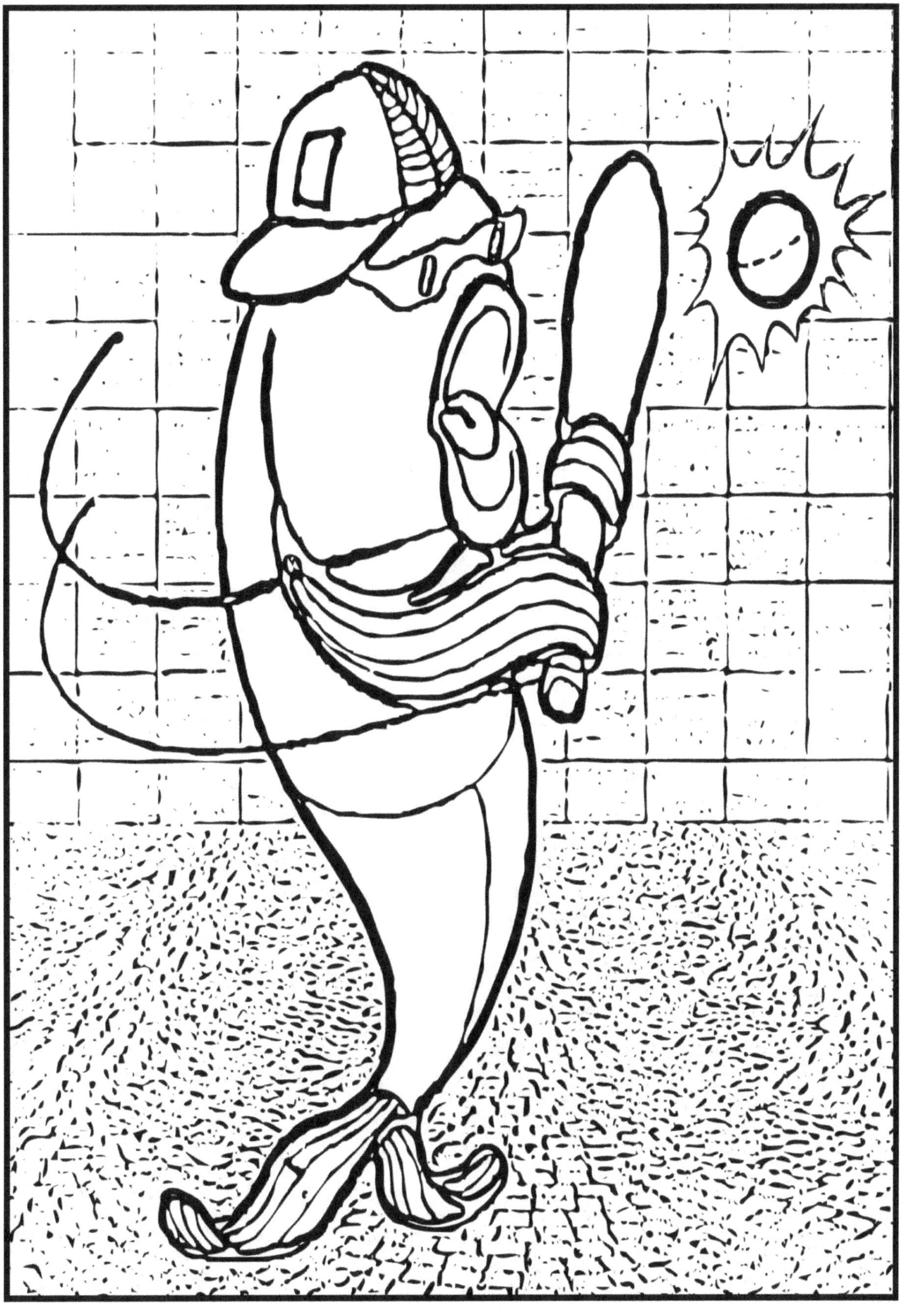

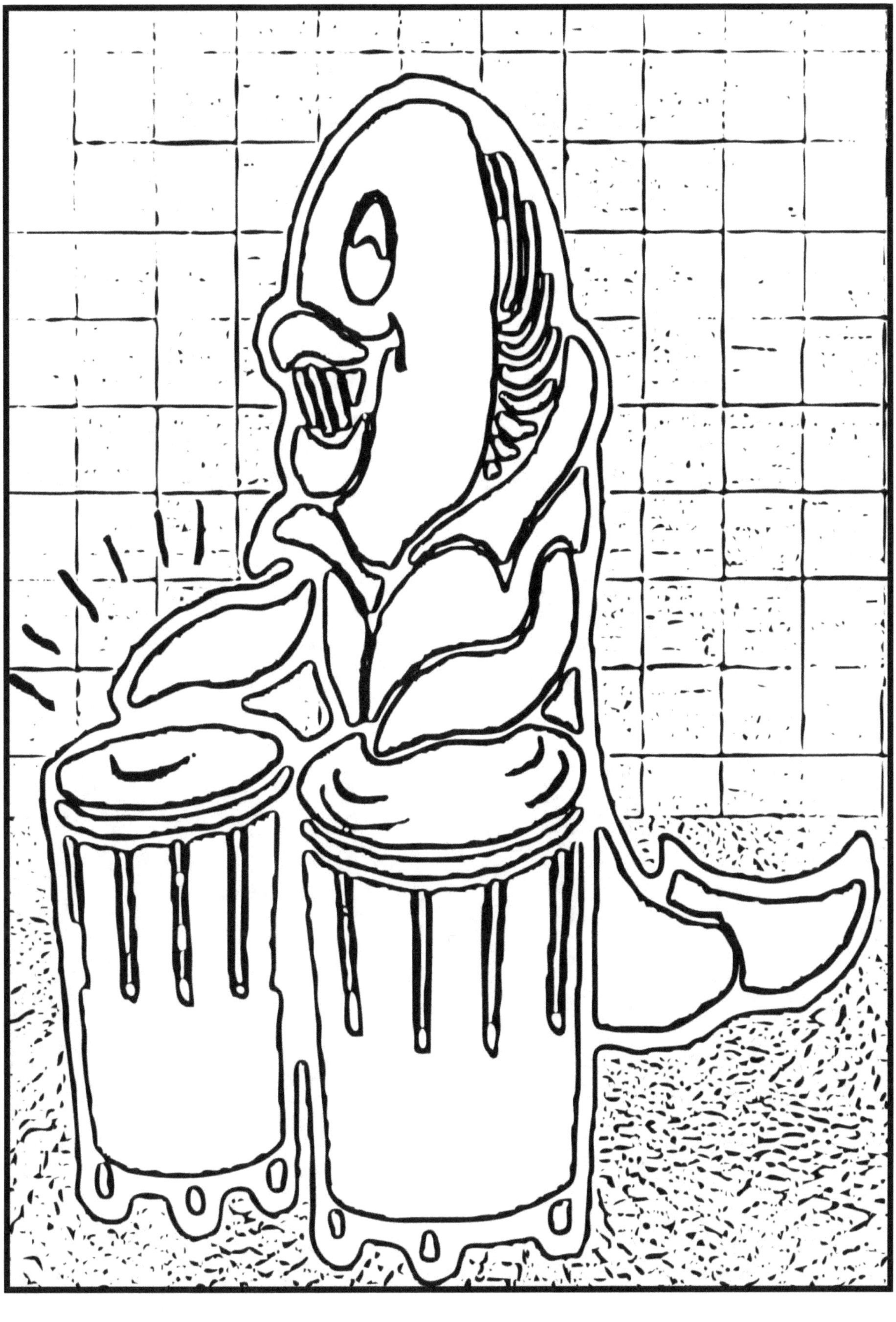

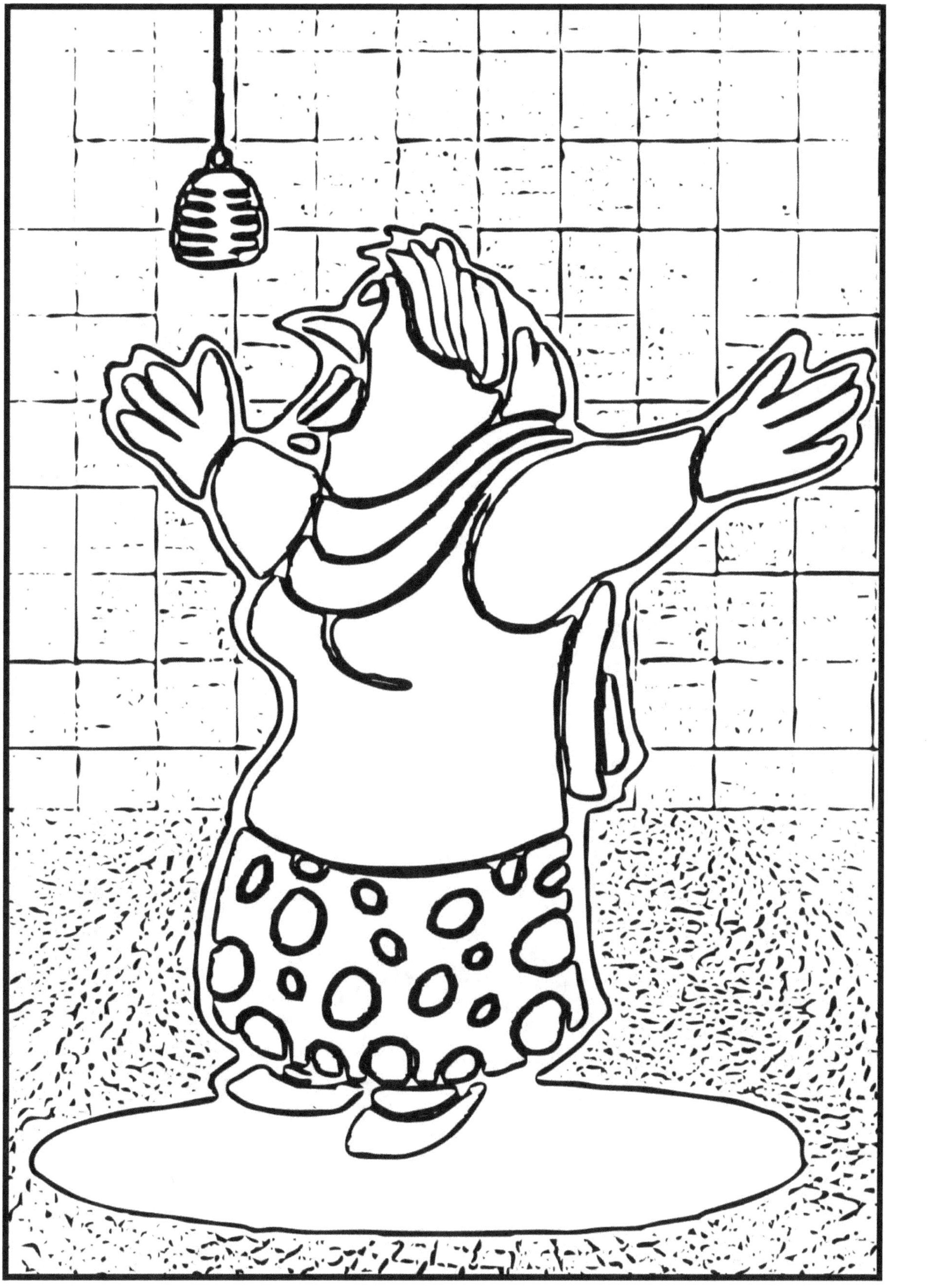

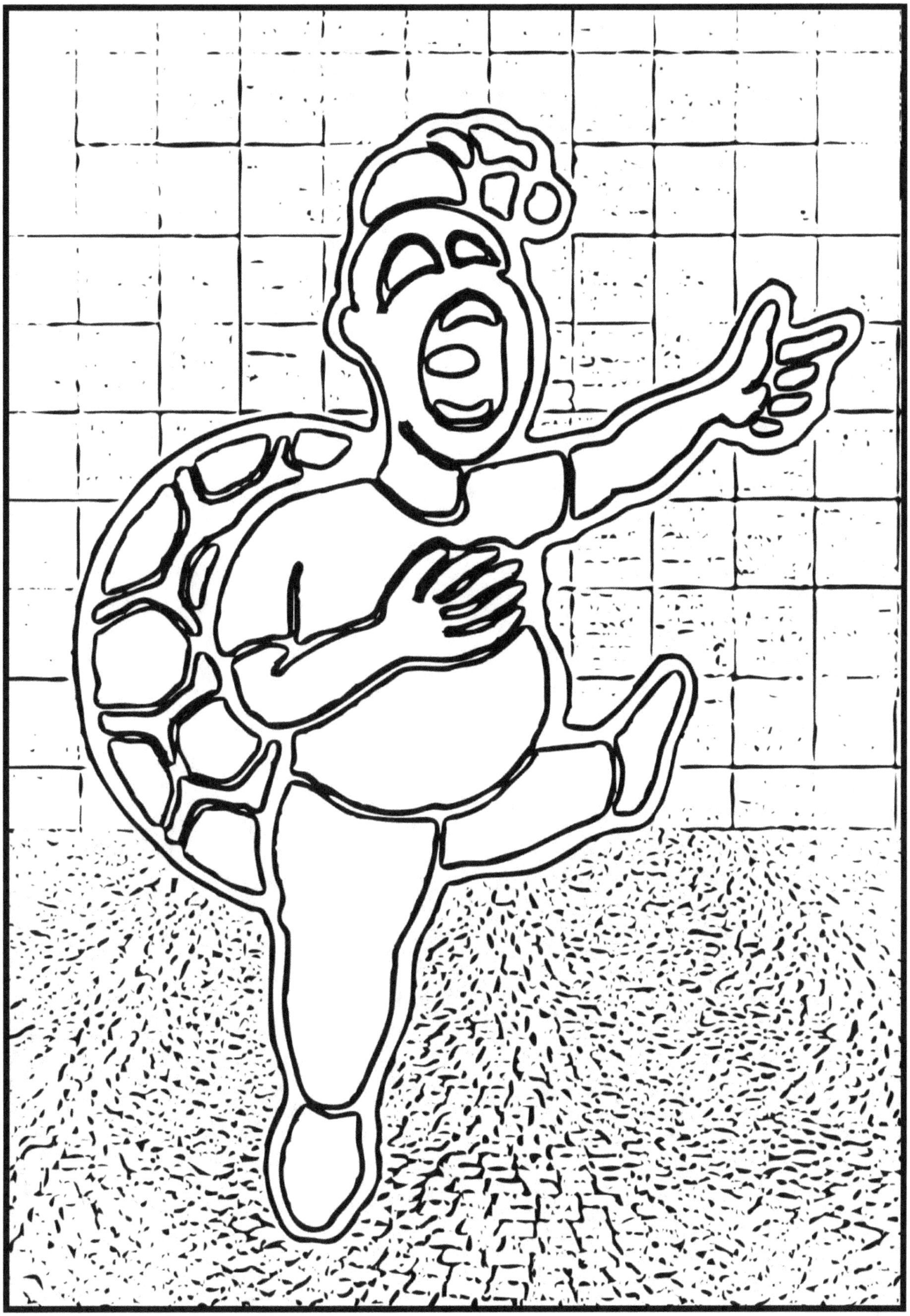

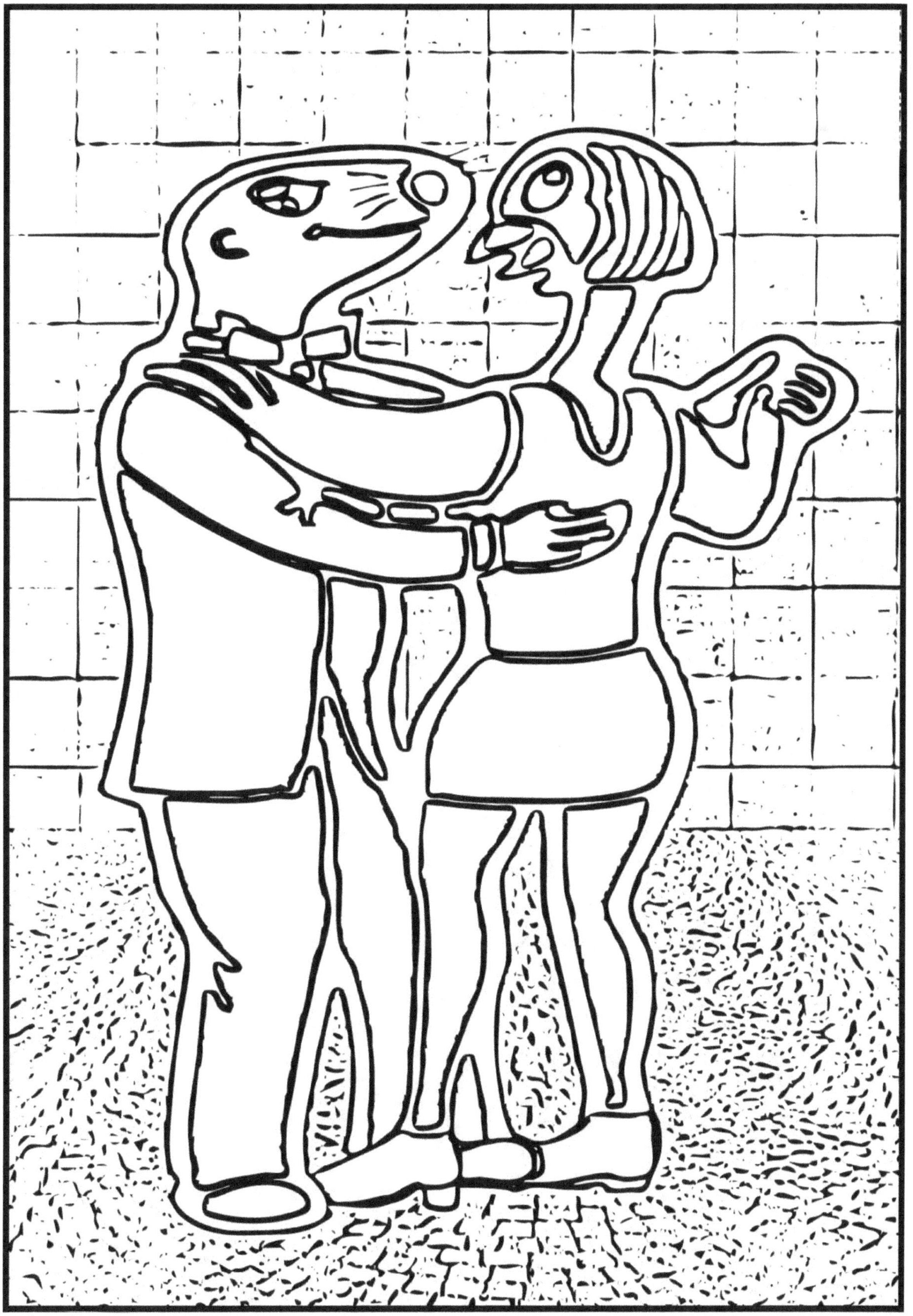

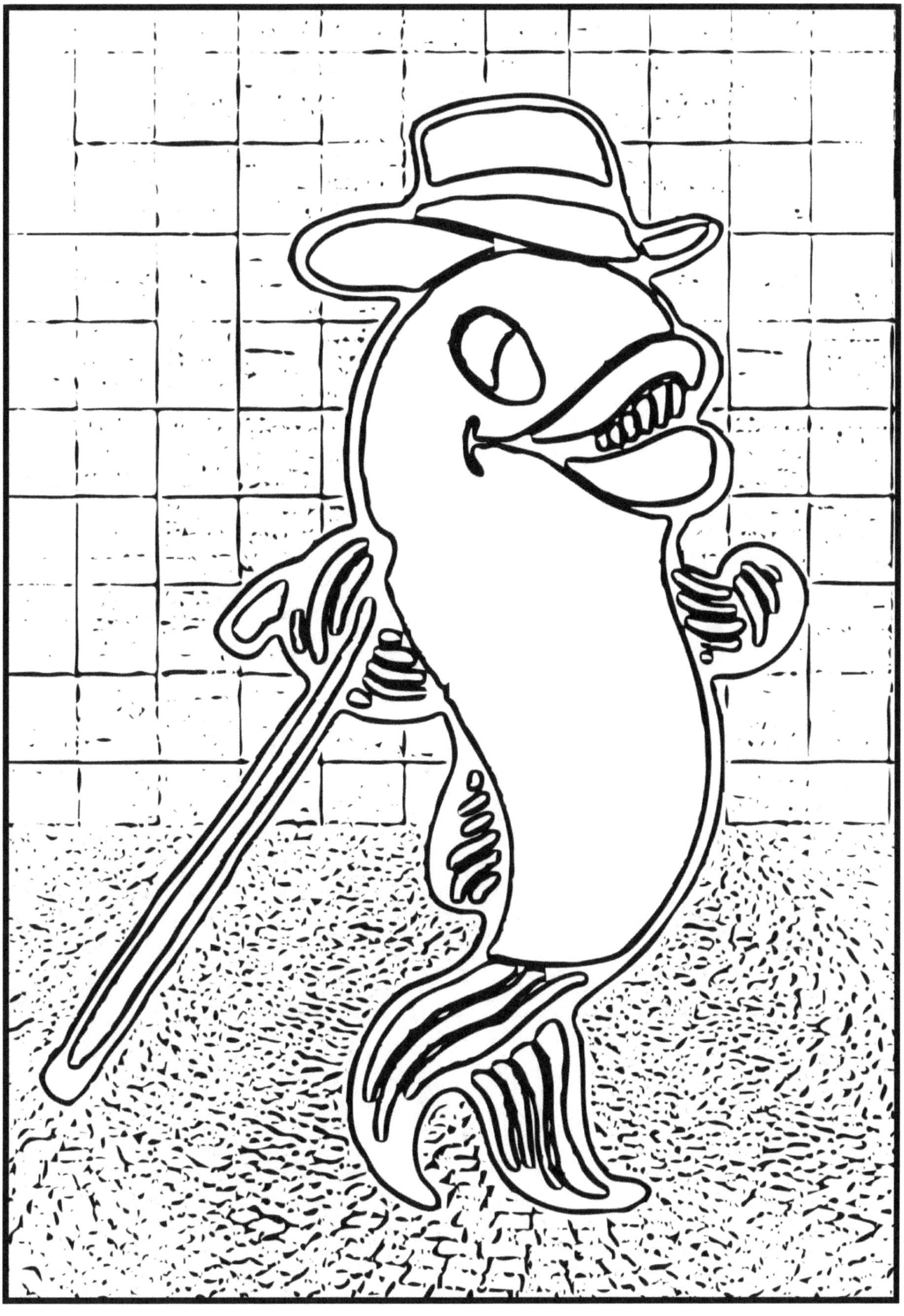

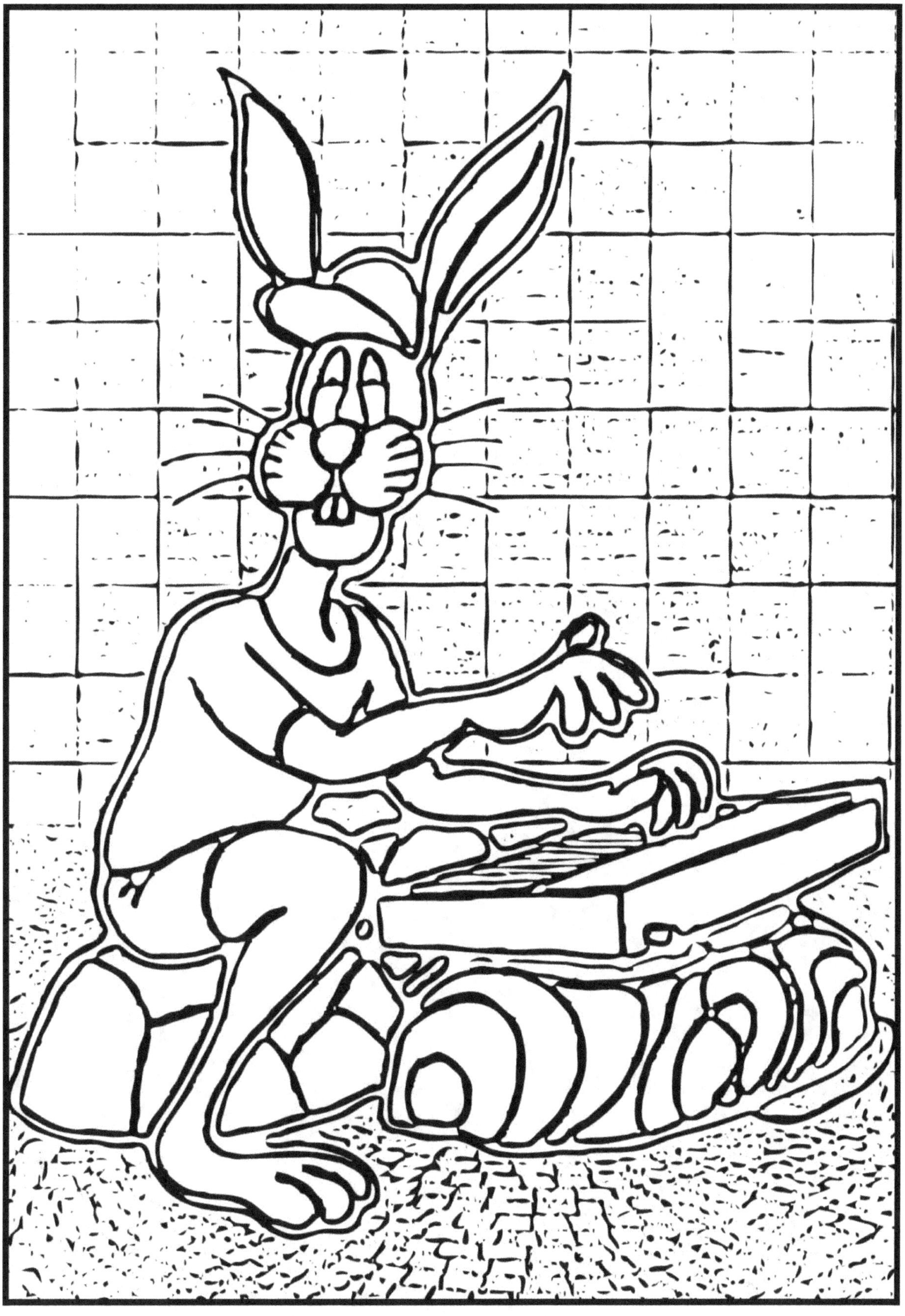

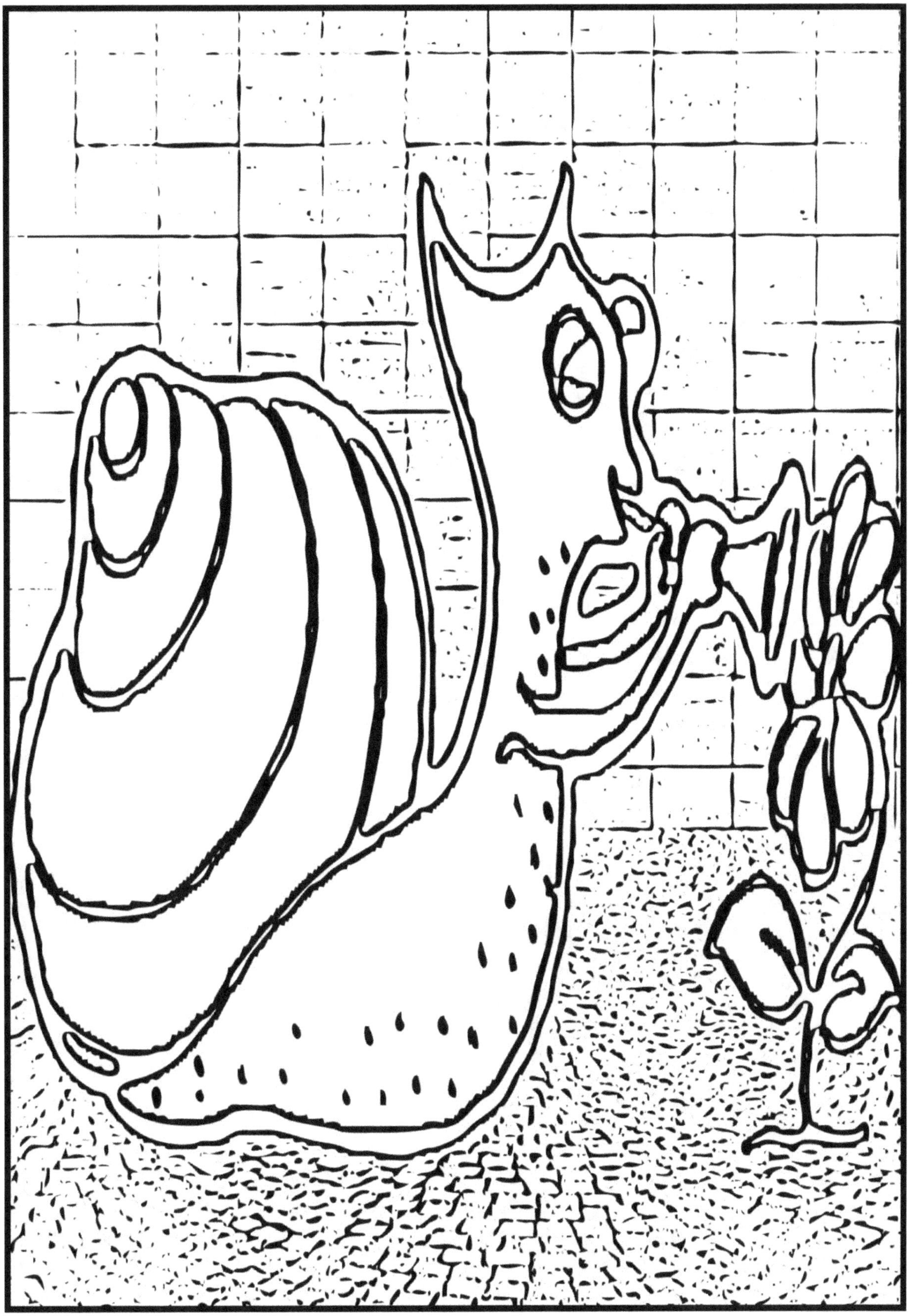

REPTILES!
Coloring Book

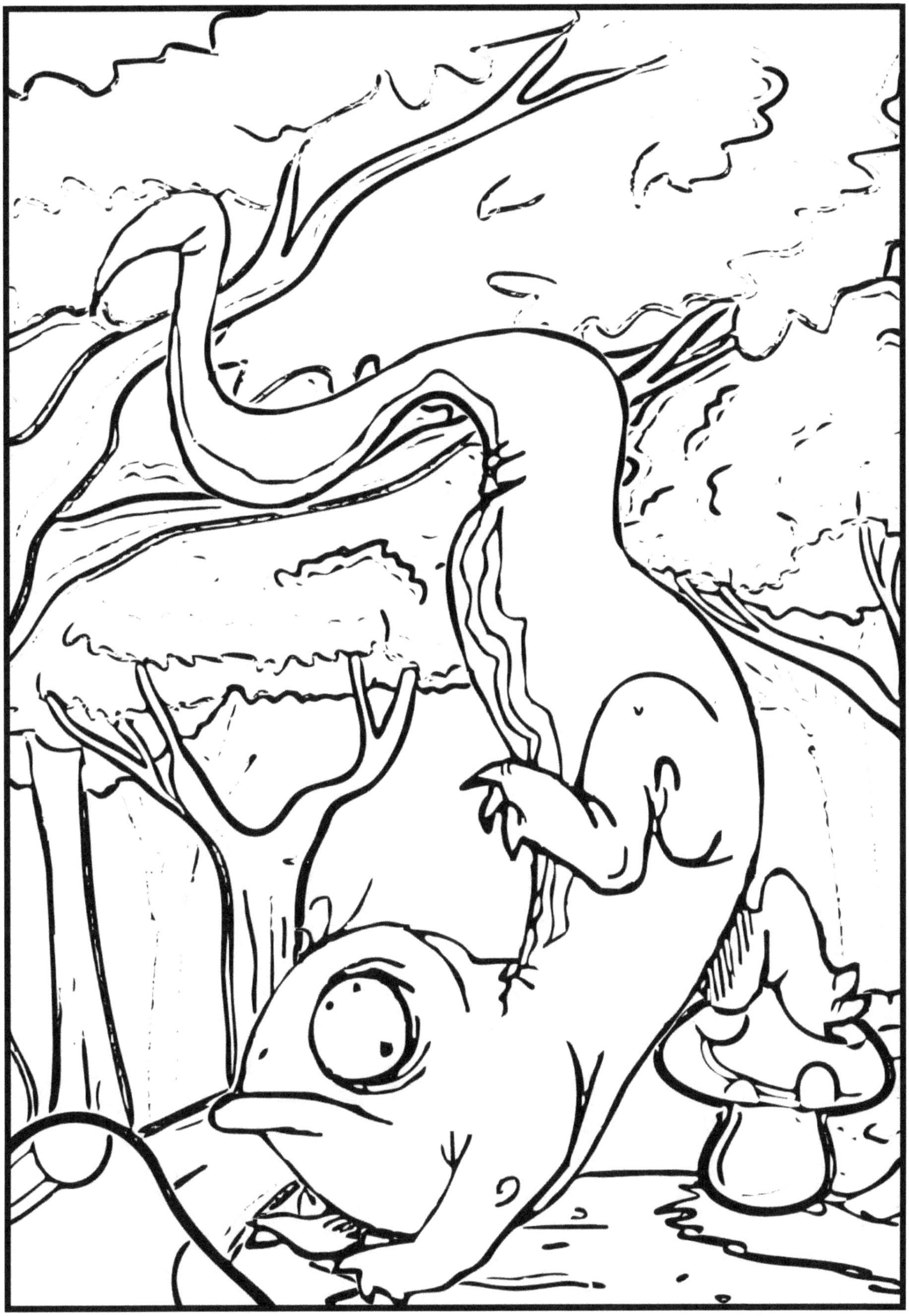

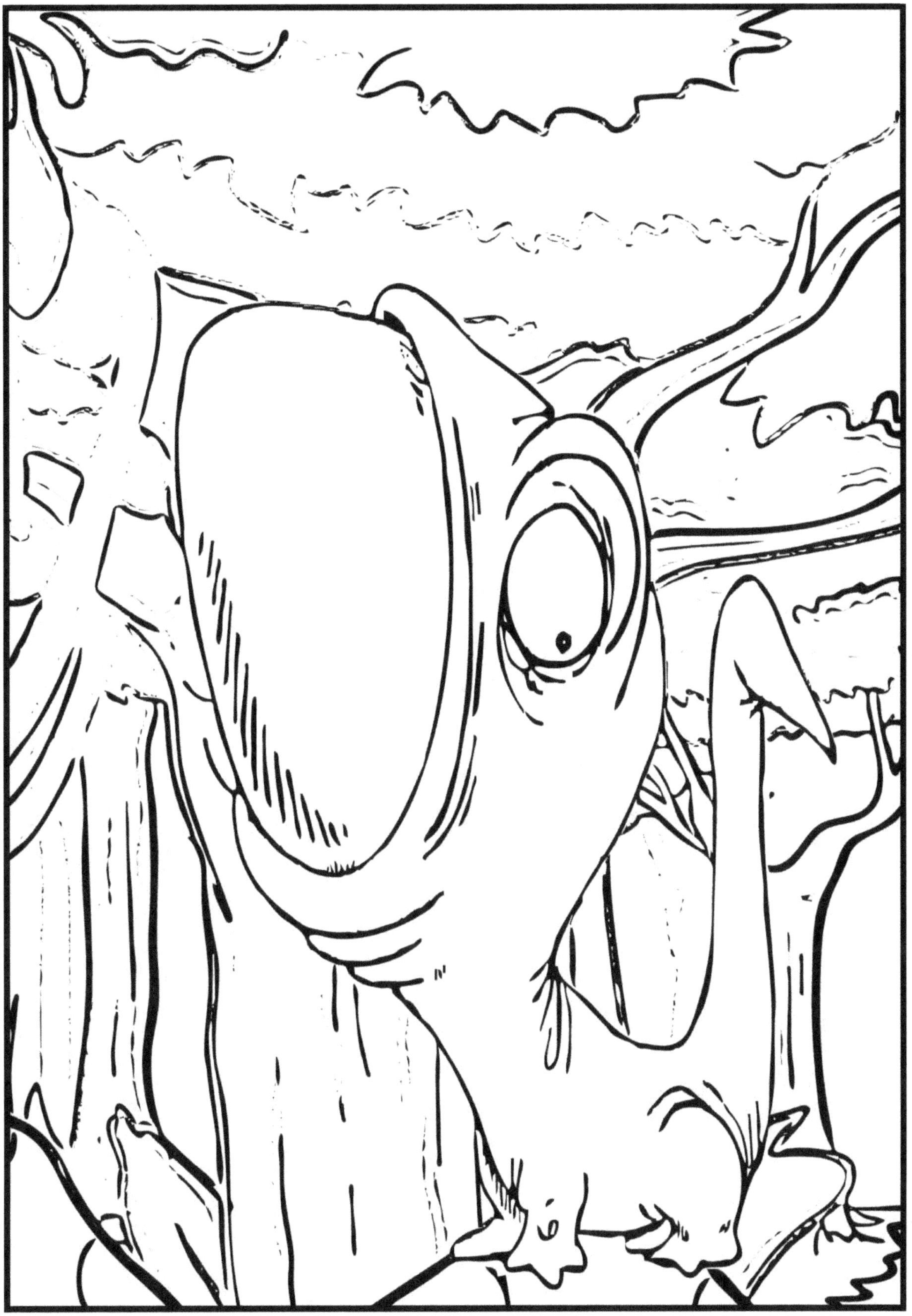

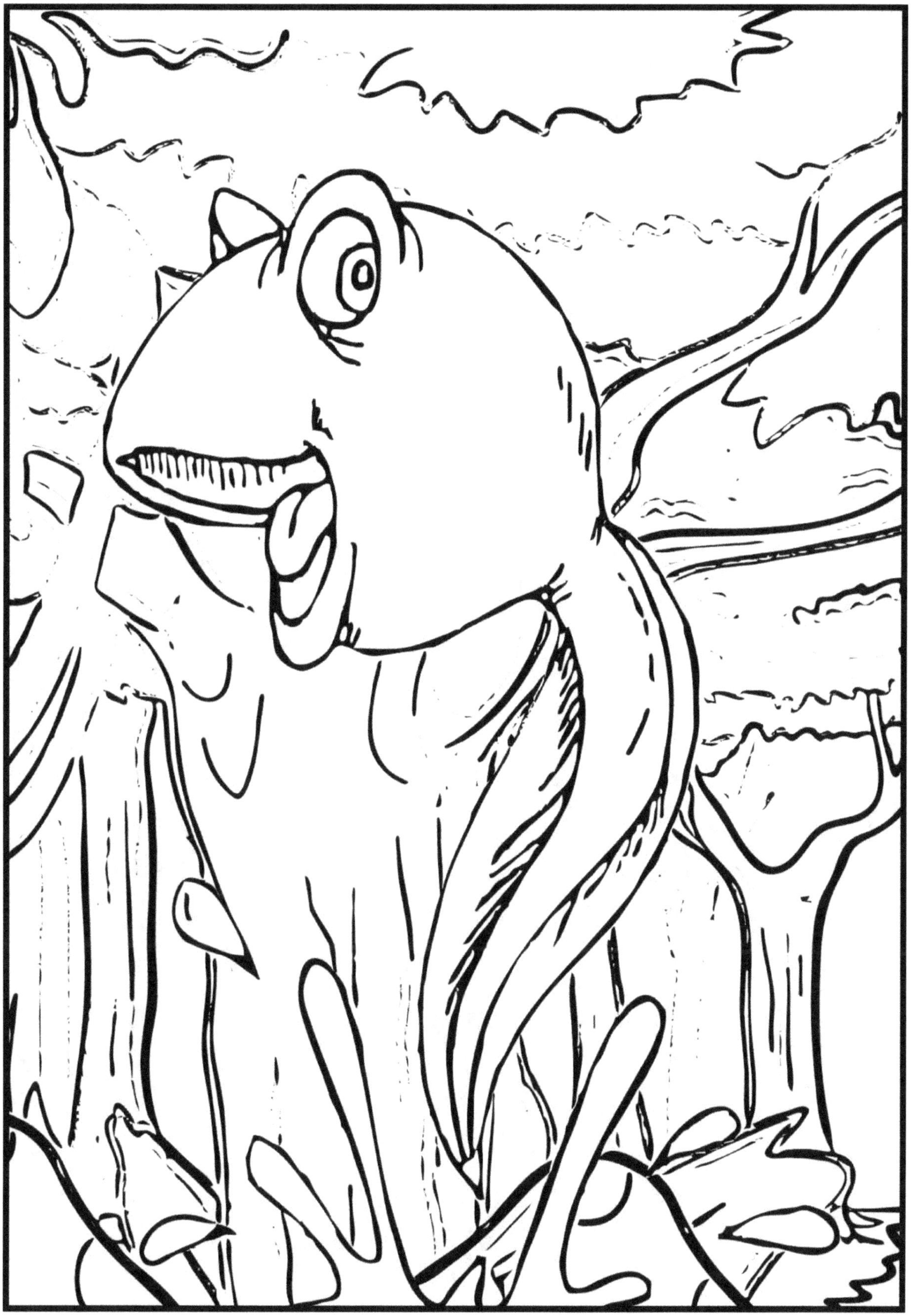

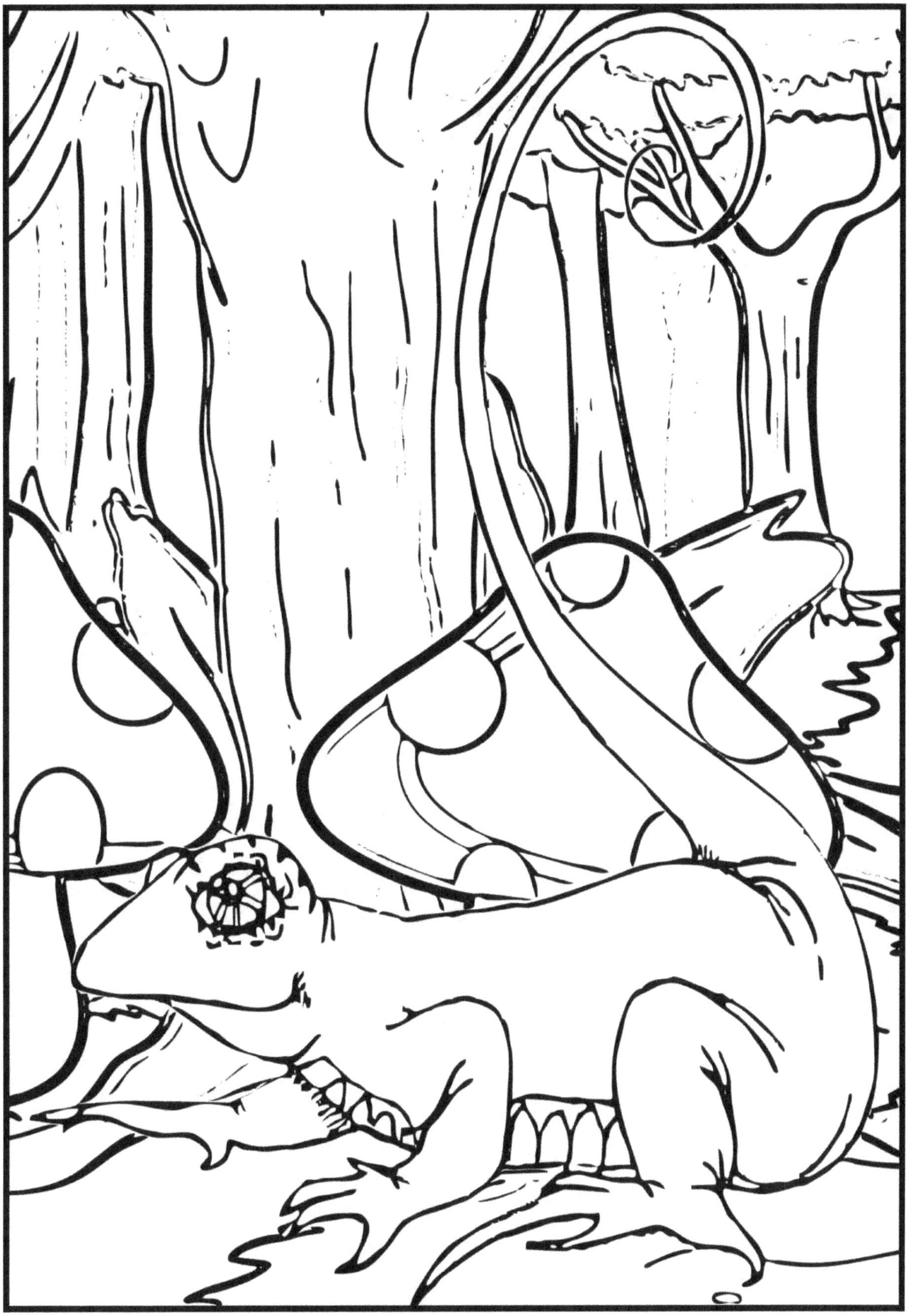

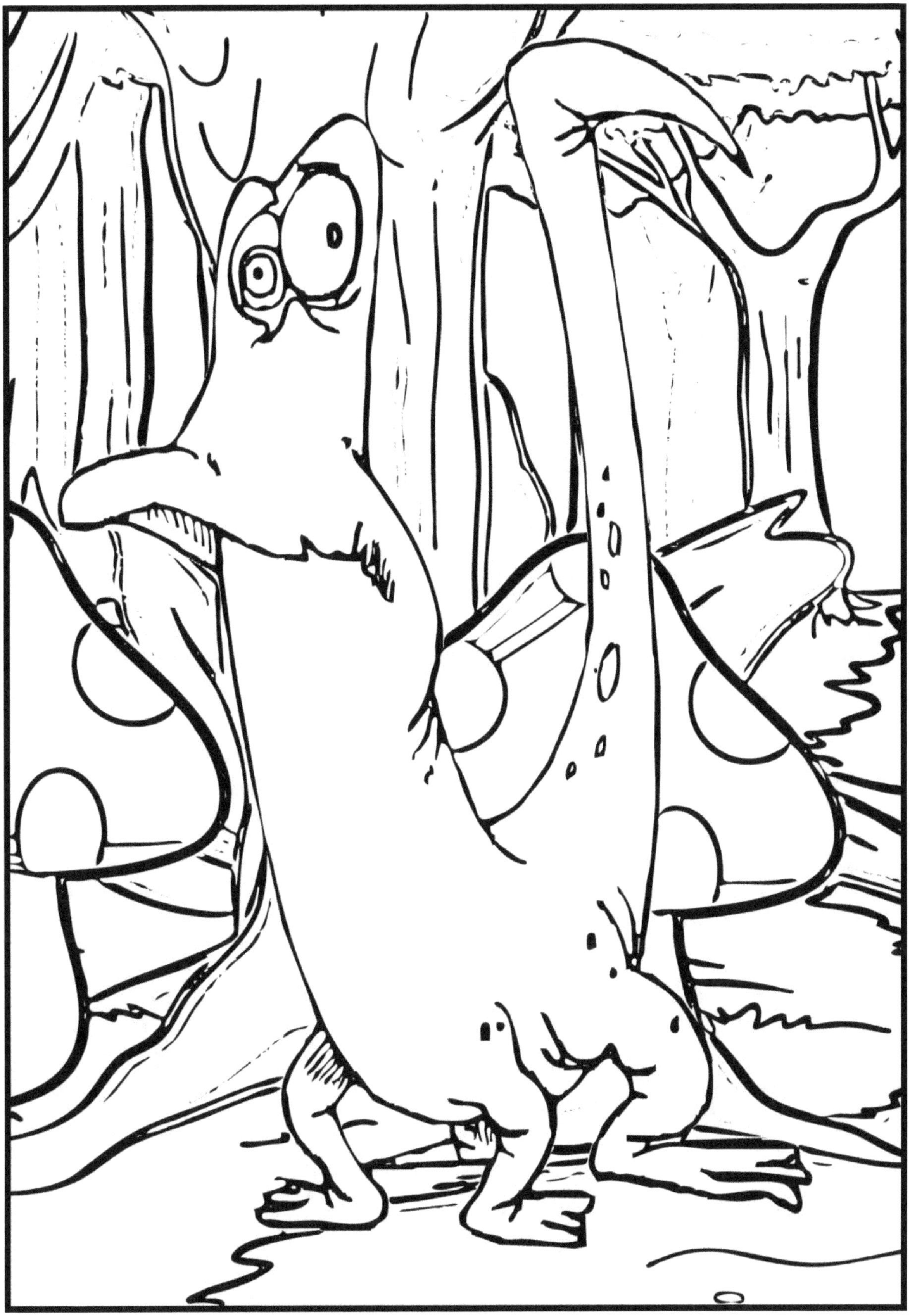

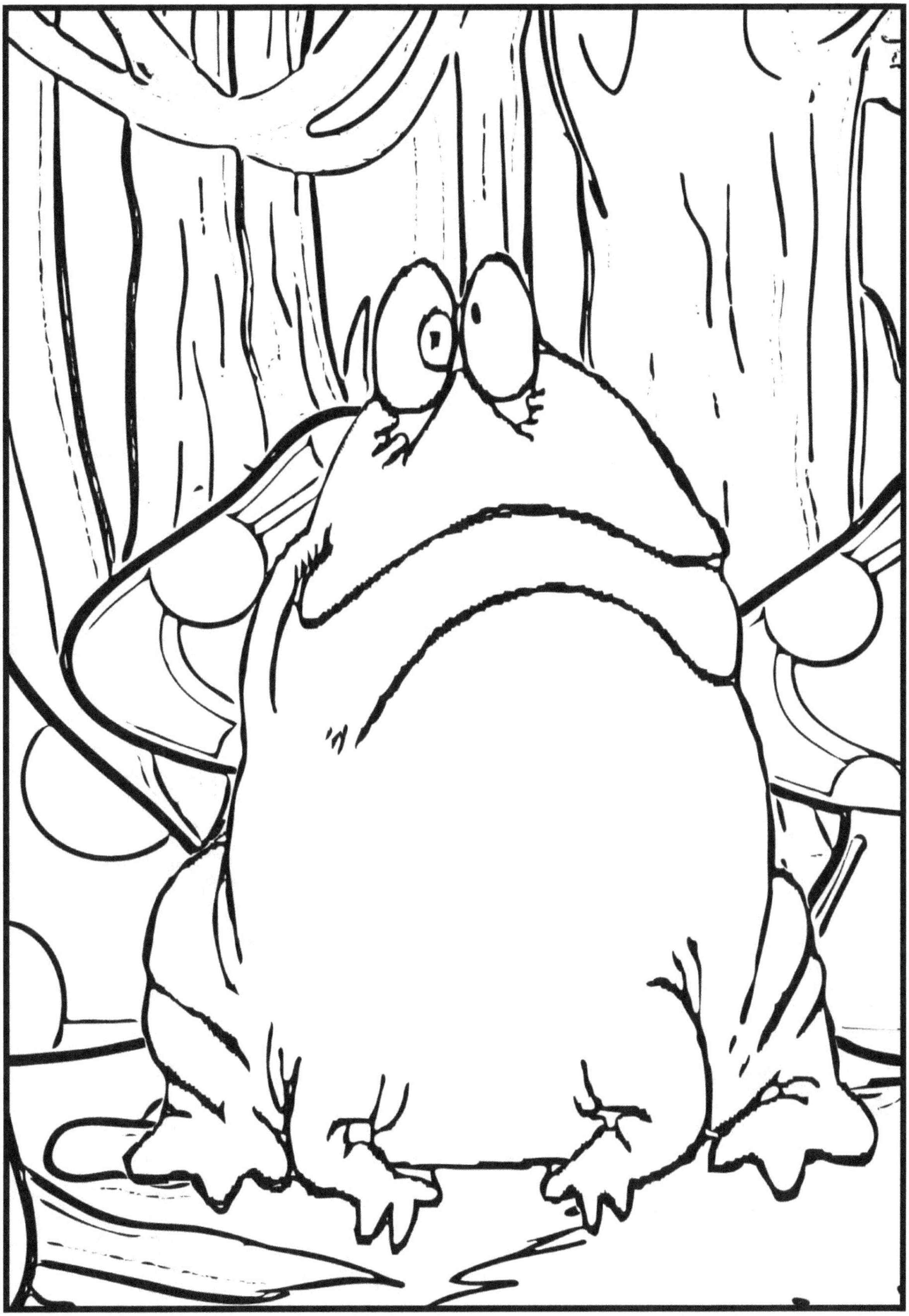

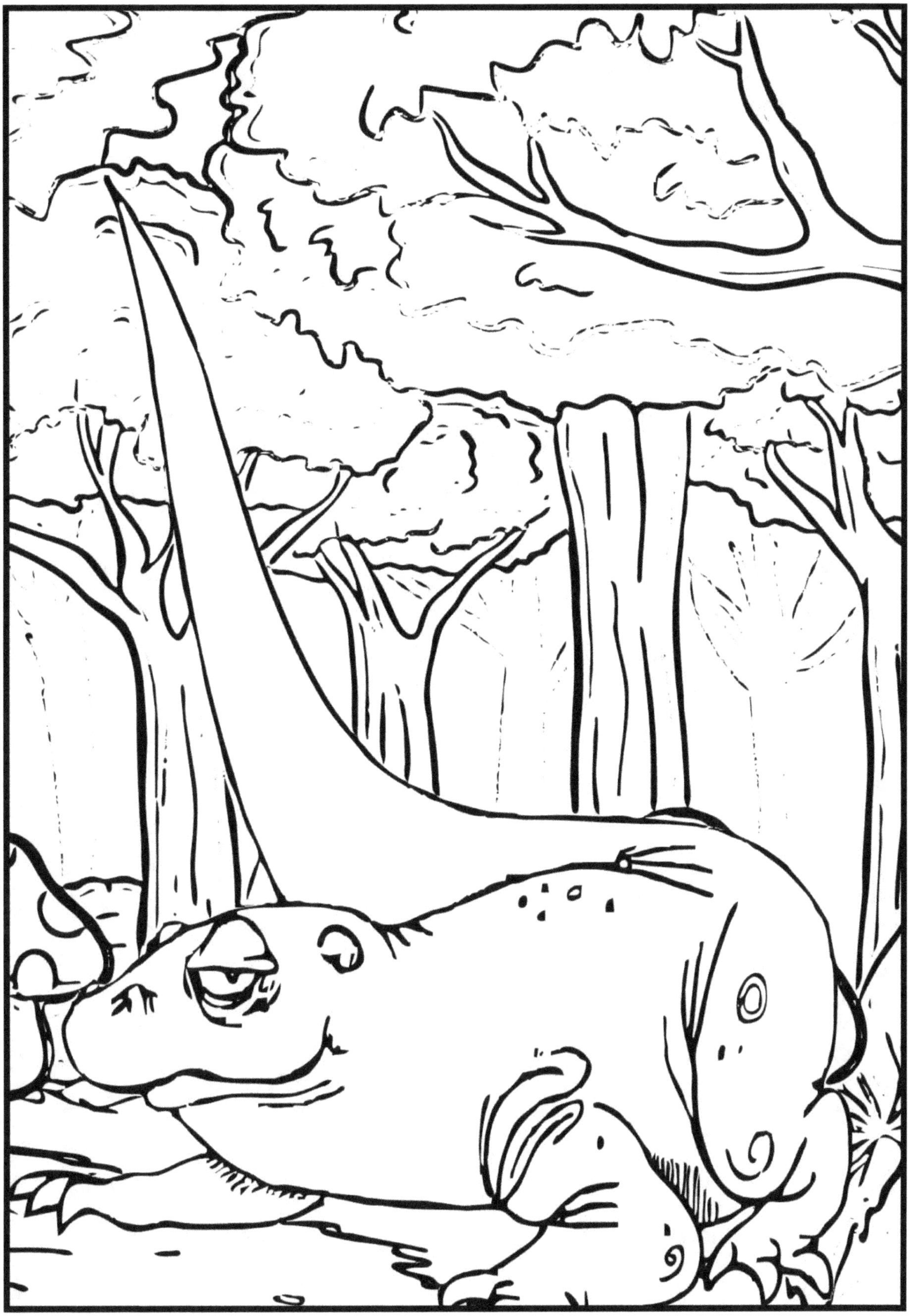

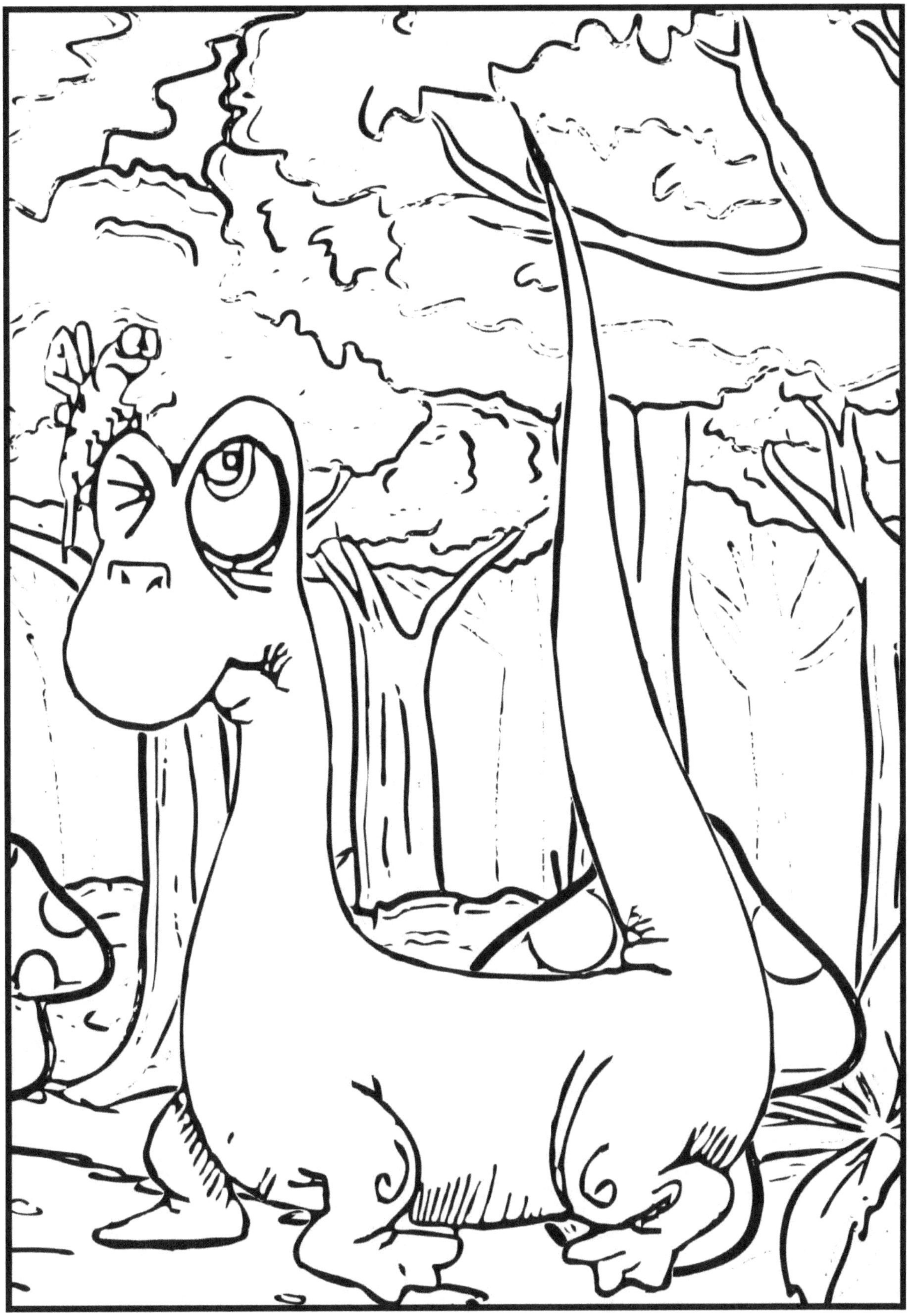

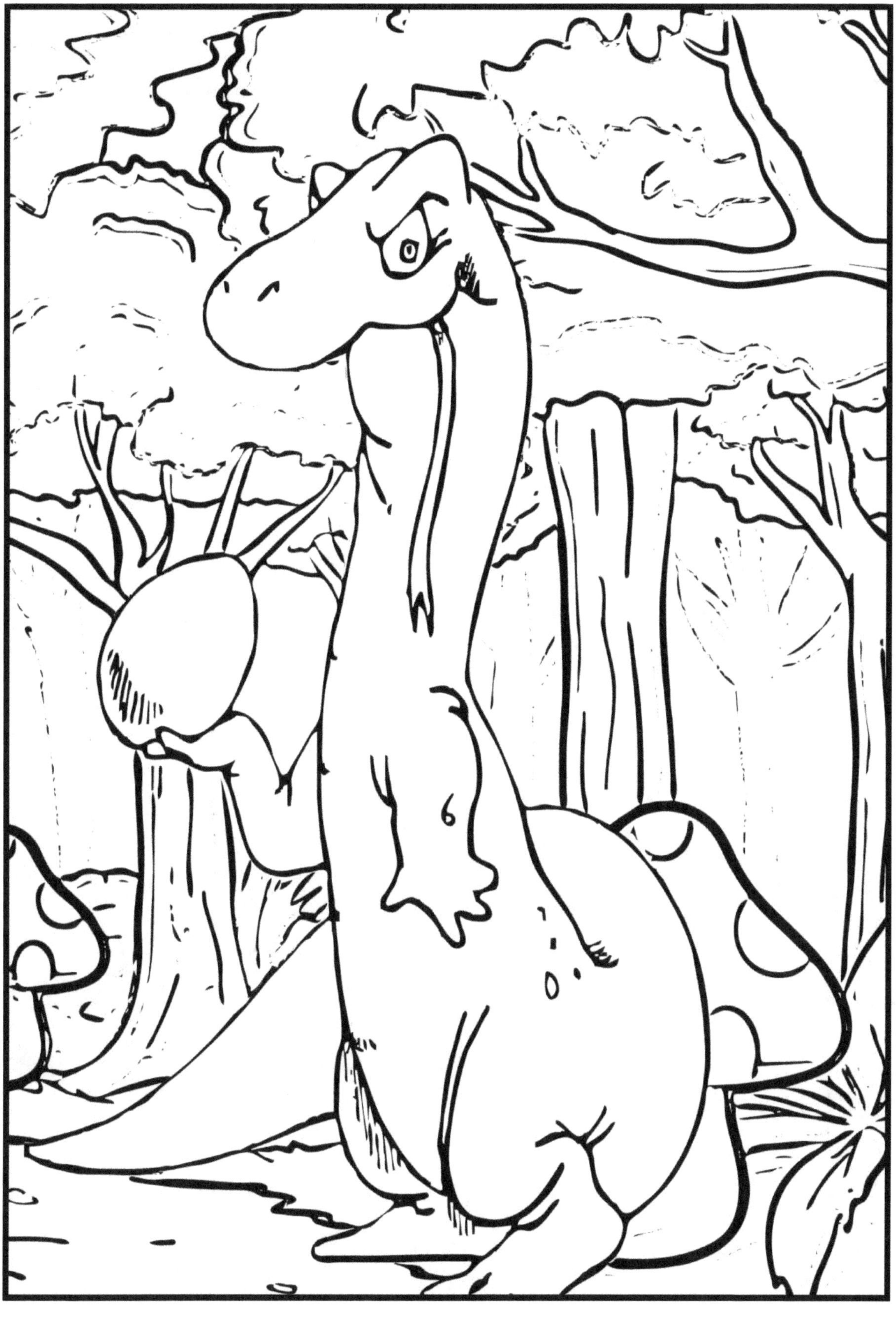

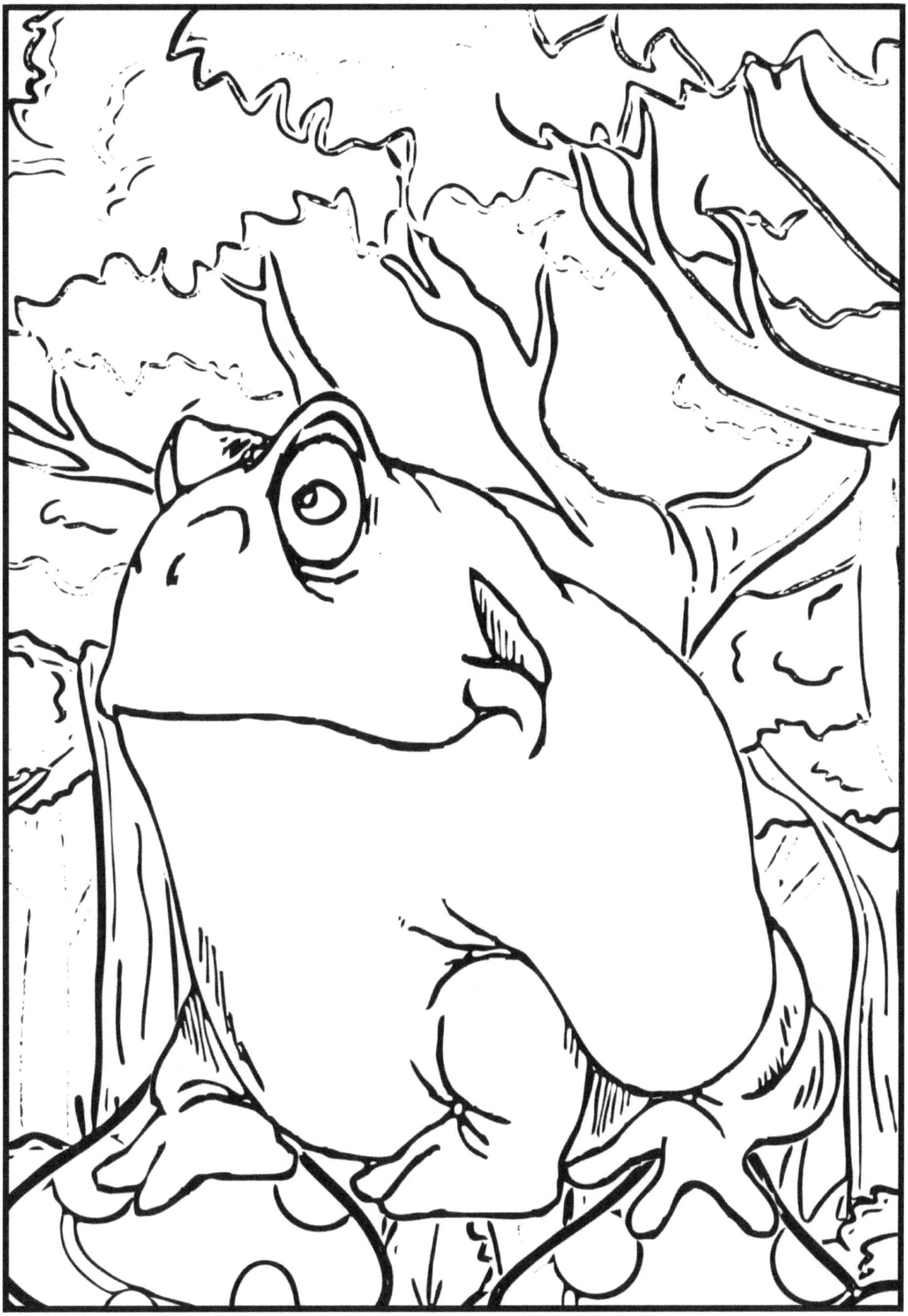

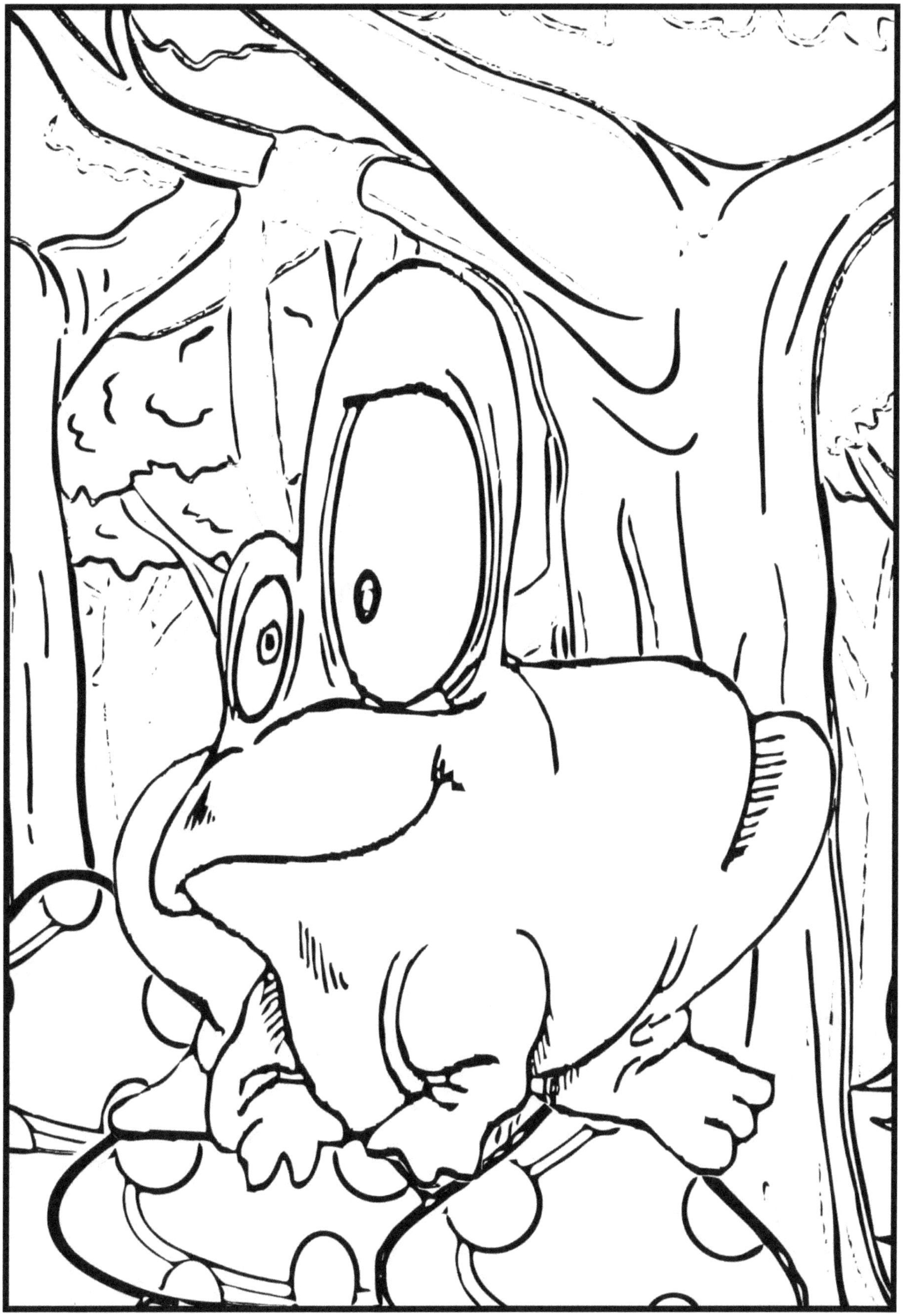

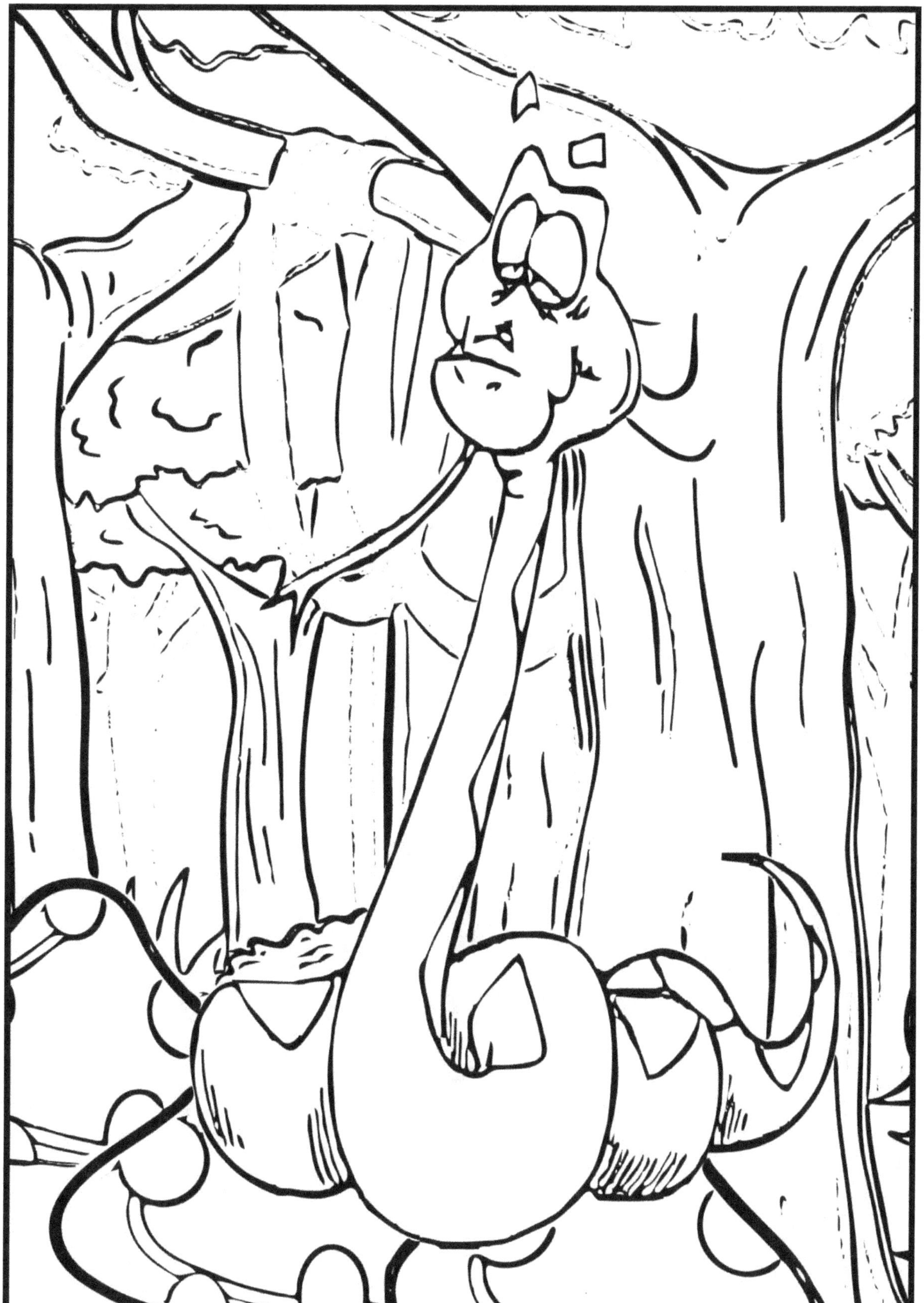

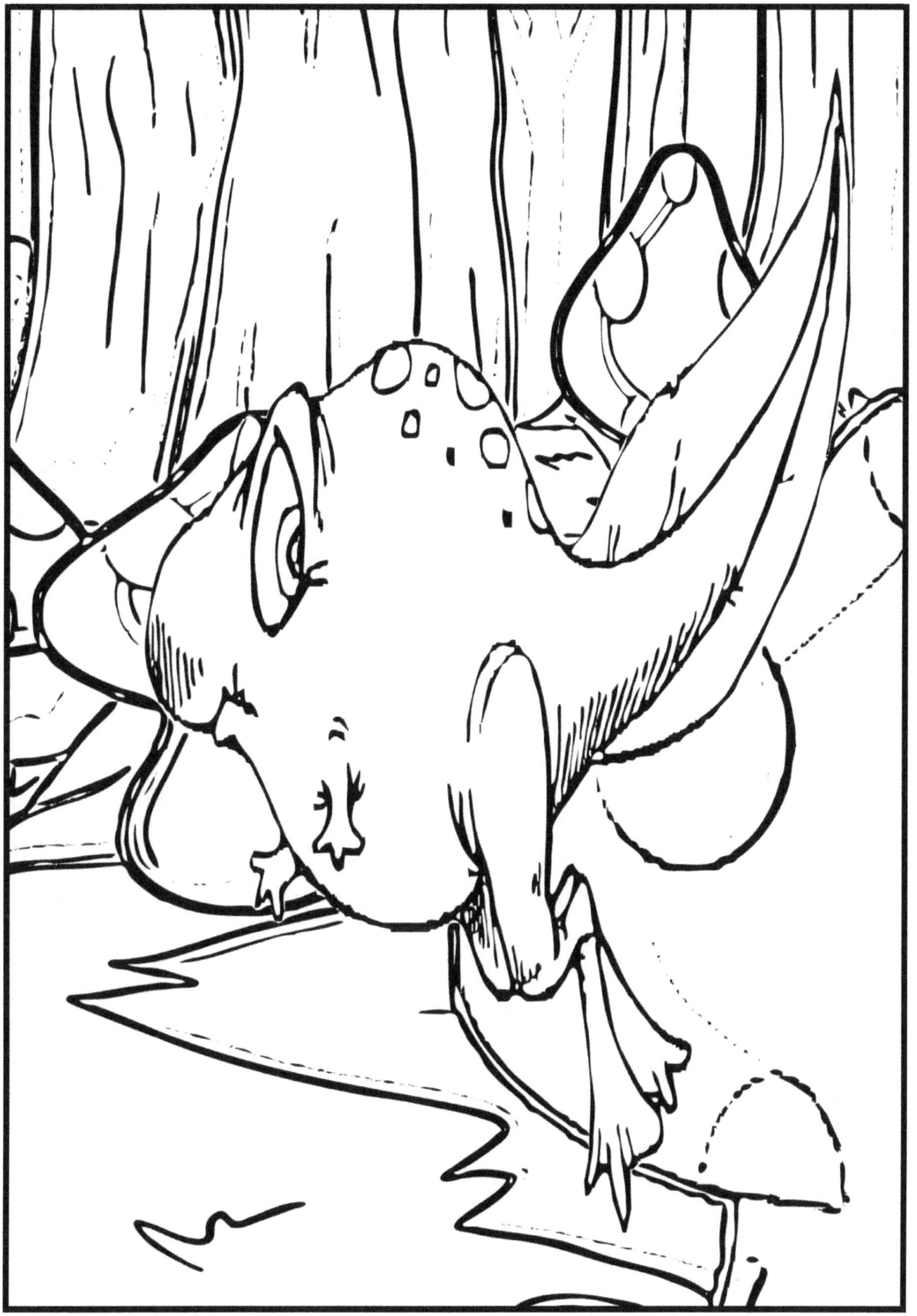

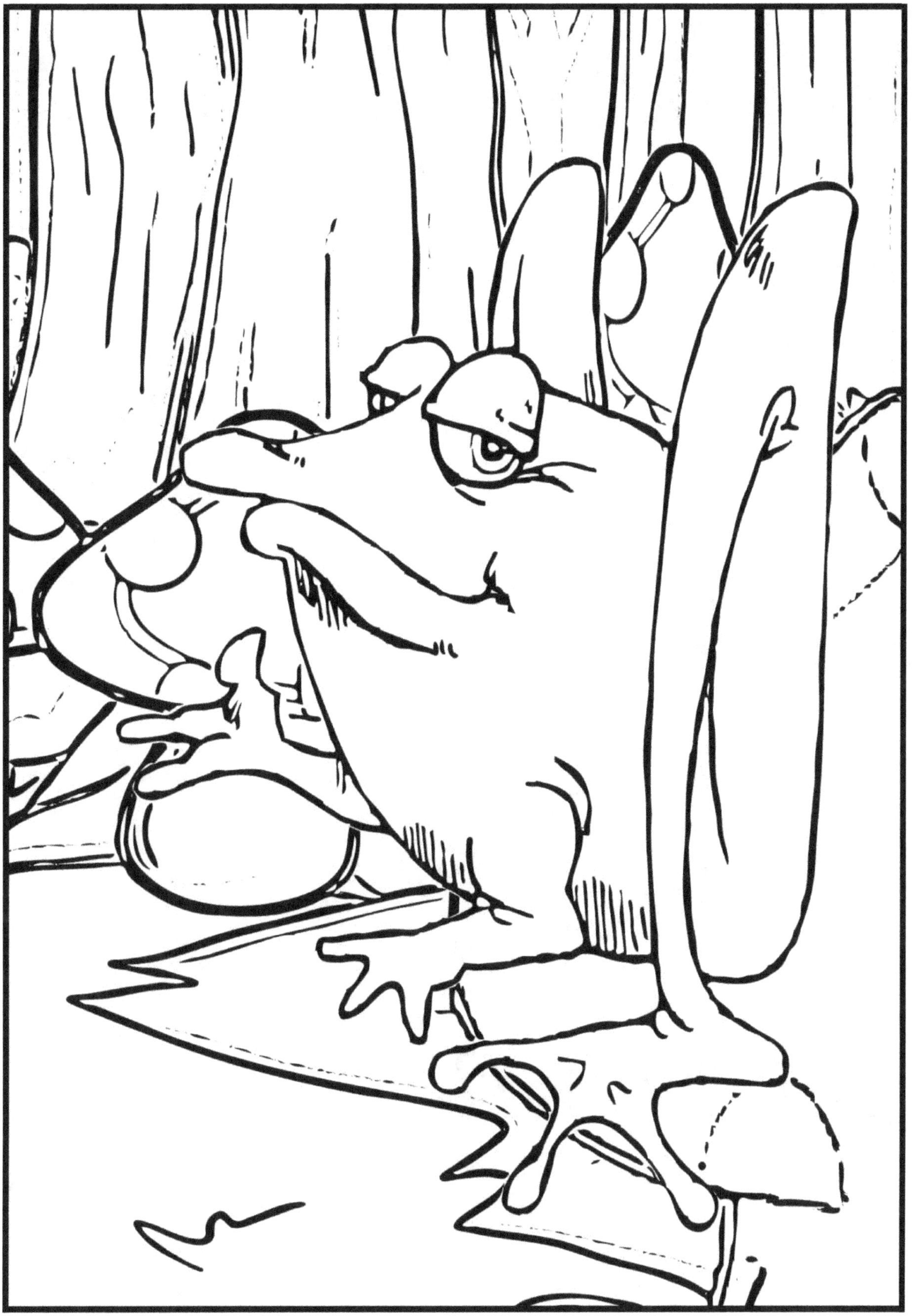

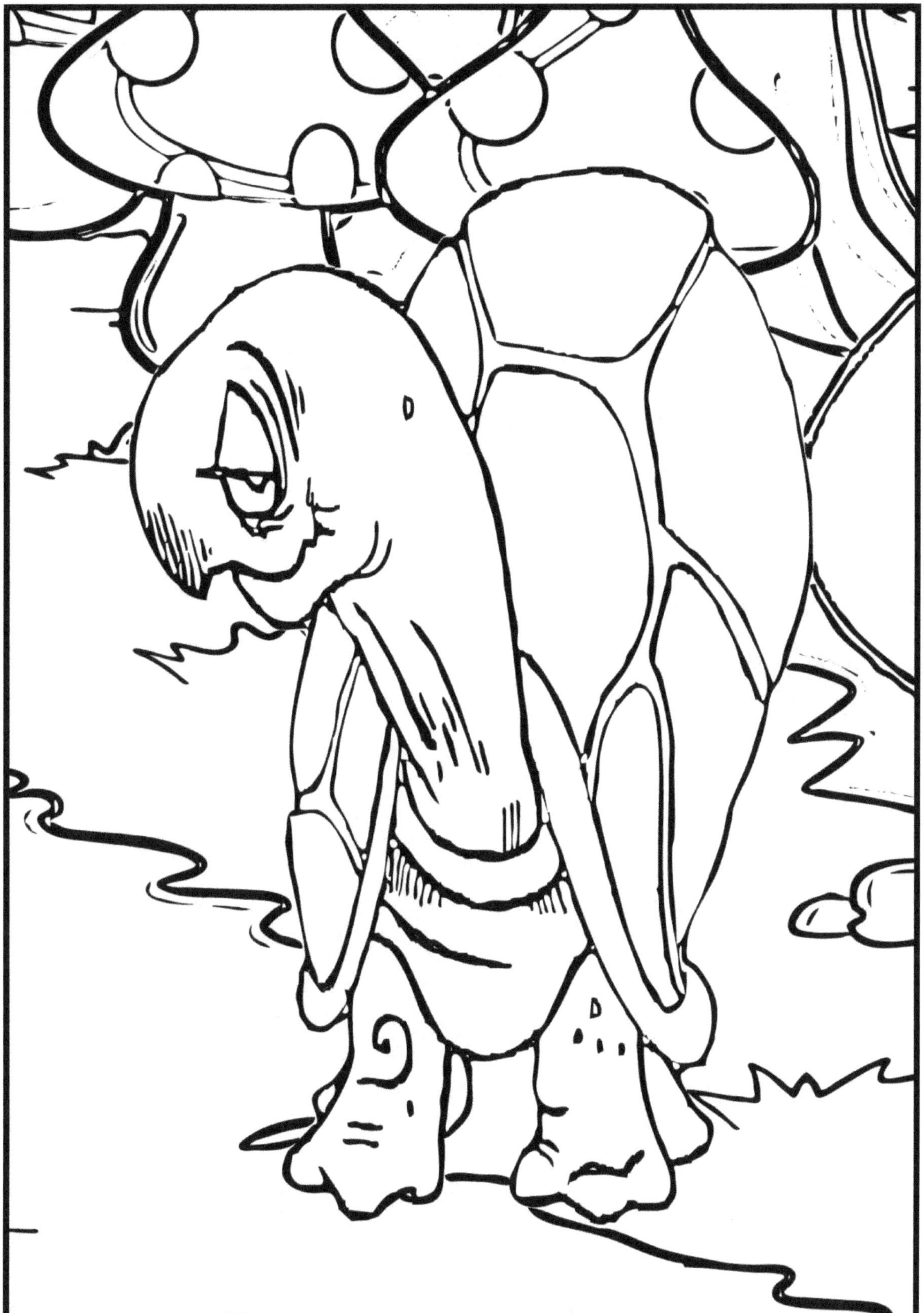

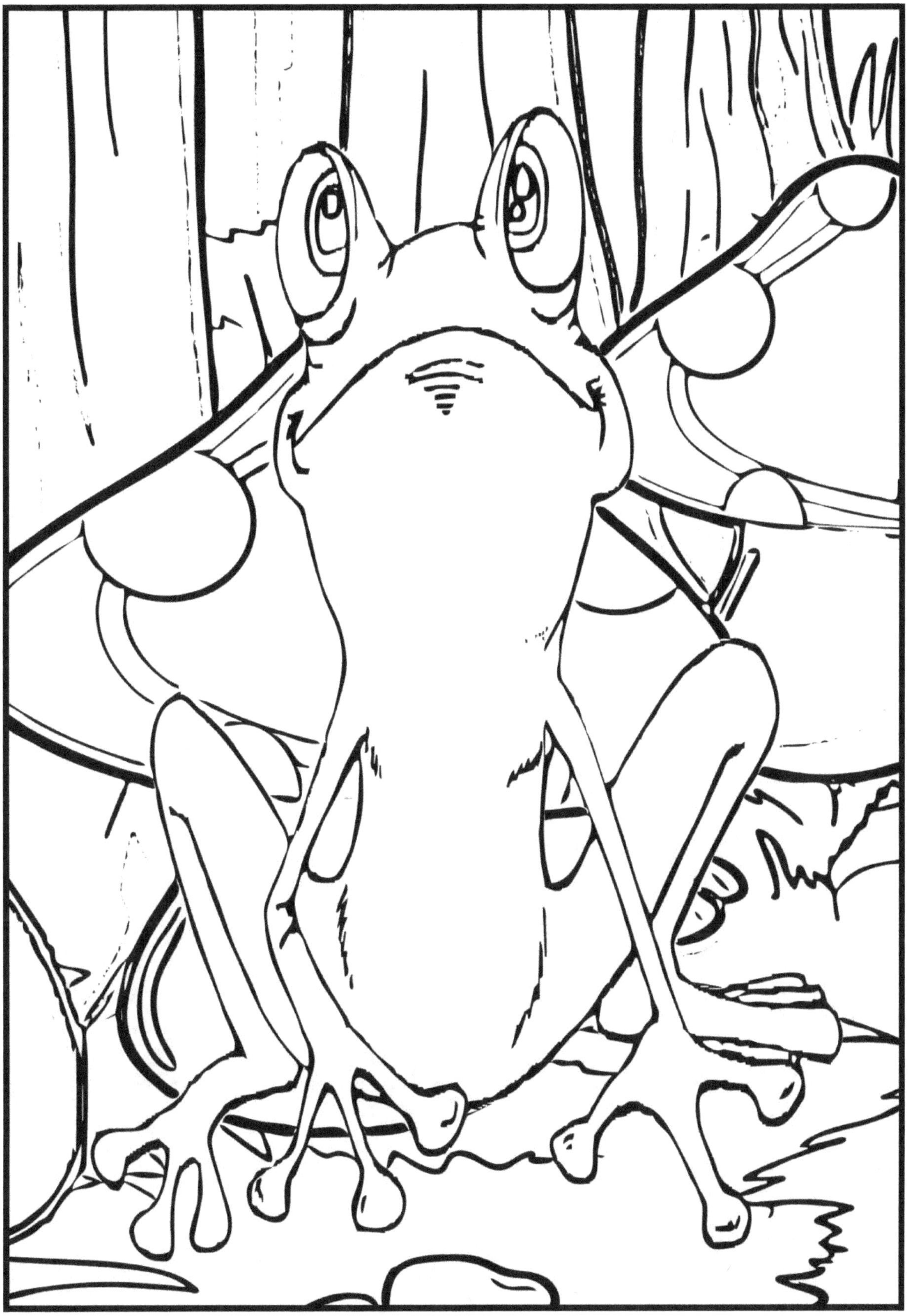

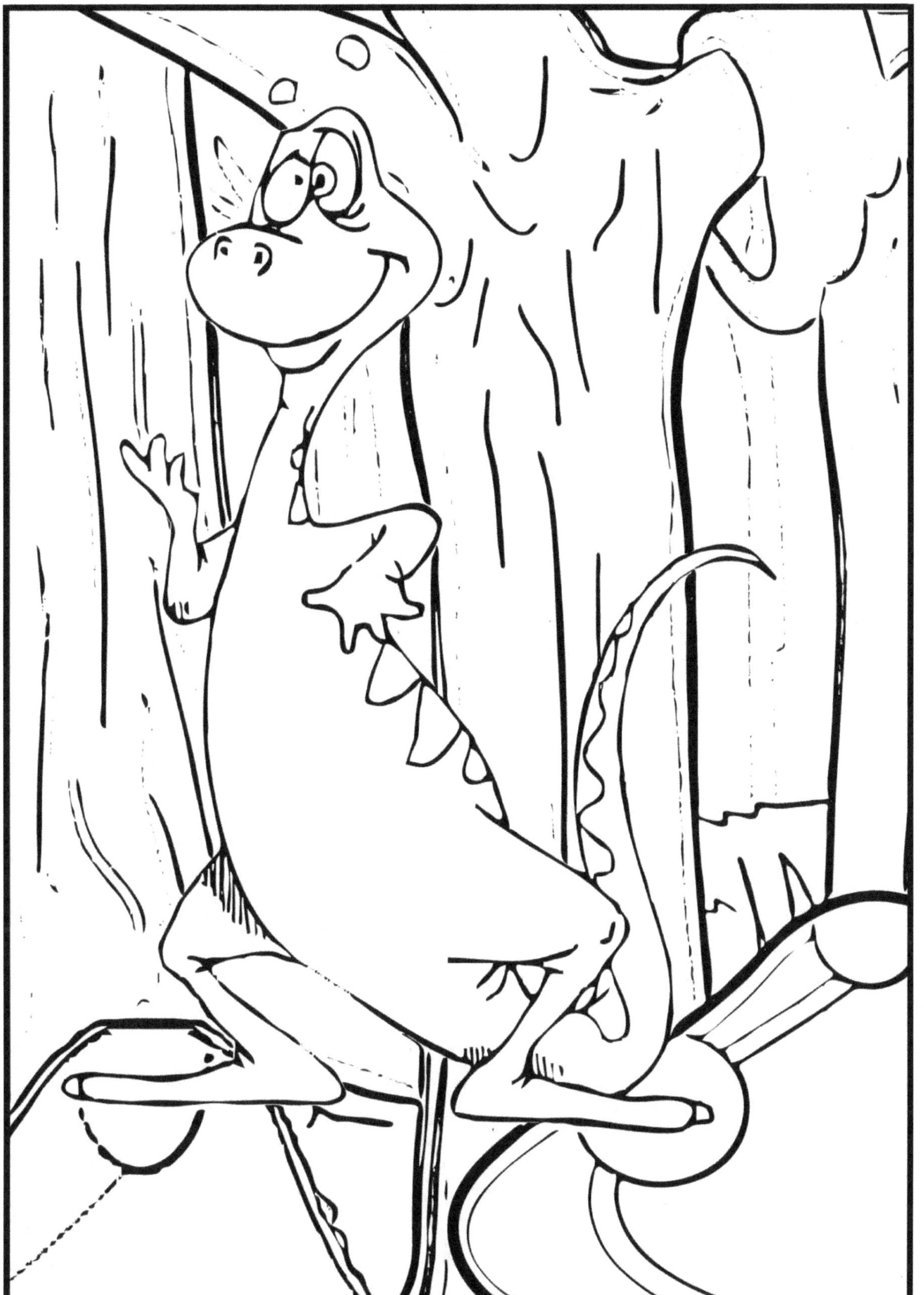

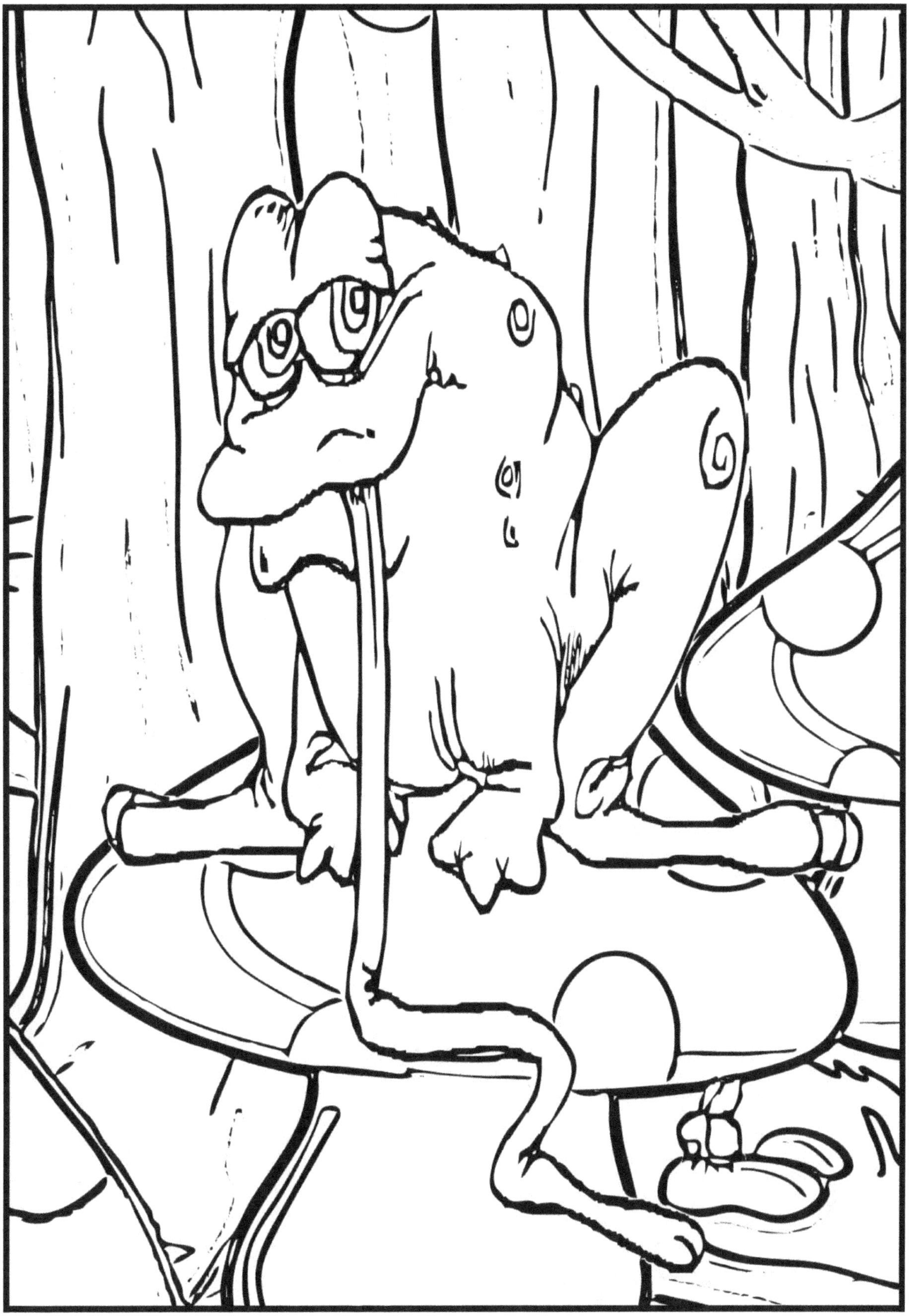

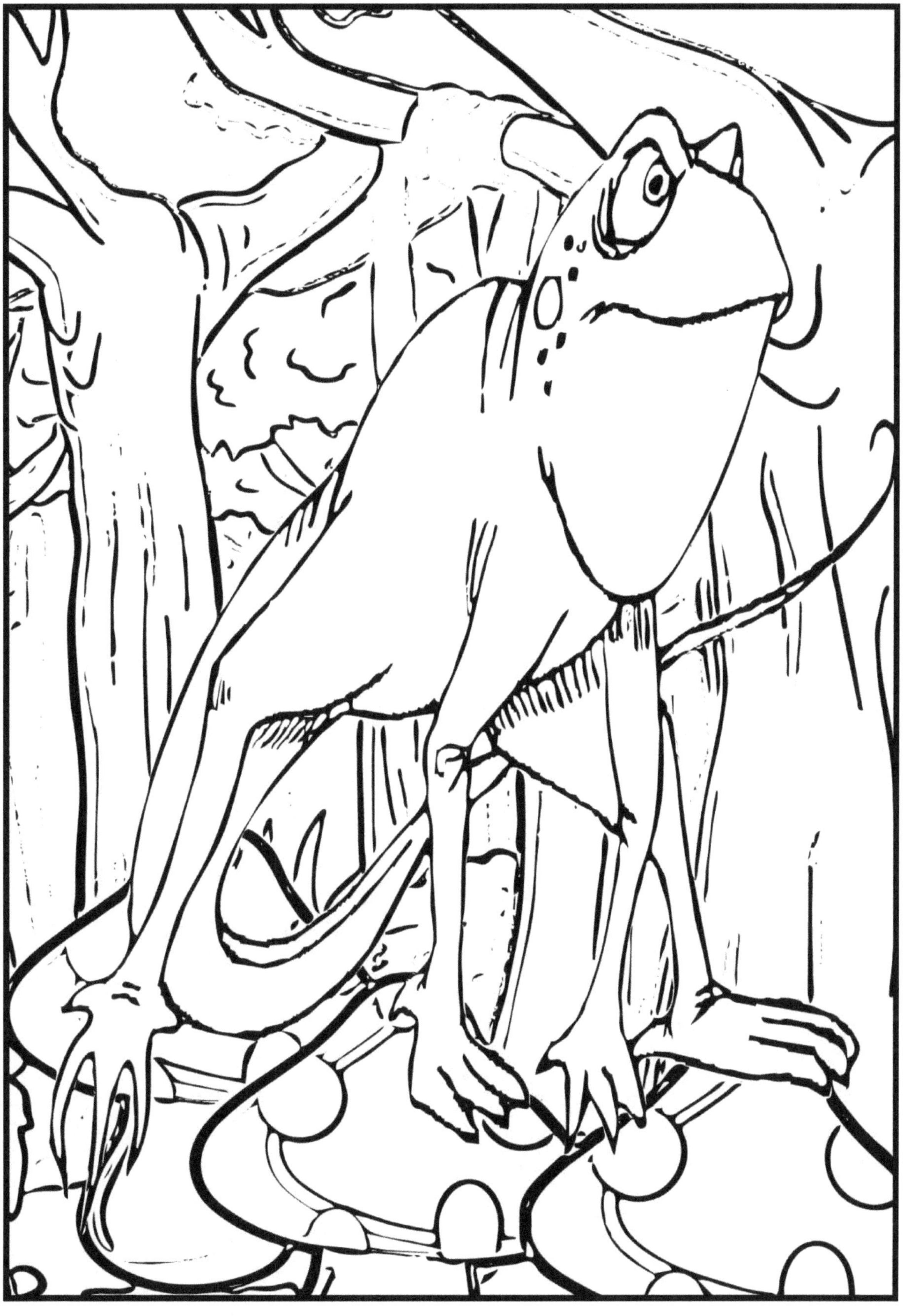

www.ingramcontent.com/pod-product-compliance
Lightning Source LLC
Chambersburg PA
CBHW081554170526
45166CB00009B/2699
9781522727033